The Health Advocate's
Basic Marketing Handbook

by
Trisha Torrey,
Every Patient's Advocate

Copyright @2014   by Trisha Torrey, Every Patient's Advocate
Previously published in 2010 as
The Health Advocate's Marketing Handbook

ISBN: 978-0-9828014-3-7

HealthAdvocateResources.com

Trisha Torrey, Every Patient's Advocate
PO Box 53
Baldwinsville, NY 13027
1-888-478-6588
contact@diagKNOWsis.com

Discounts for bulk-orders of this book are available by contacting the author.
Trisha Torrey is also available for speaking opportunities to groups of patients or
professionals.

DiagKNOWsis Media
PO Box 53
Baldwinsville, NY 13027
www.DiagKNOWsis.com

Also from DiagKNOWsis Media:

♦ You Bet Your Life! The 10 Mistakes Every Patient Makes
  (How to Fix Them to Get the Healthcare You Deserve)
♦ The Health Advocate's Start and Grow Your Own Practice Handbook
♦ The Health Advocate's Advanced Marketing Handbook (mid-2014)

Printed in the United States of America

Dedication

Health and patient advocates are my heroes.
They have dedicated their careers to assisting
people who otherwise could not get the
medical system related assistance they need.

So I dedicate this book to "my" advocates—those
who are members of the Alliance of Professional
Health Advocates — which helps them help even
more people.

Thanks to you all,
from the bottom of
my heart.

Table of Contents

Introduction

I love that you have purchased this book, but probably not for the reason you think.

If you think it's because I'll make my fortune, then you're mistaken. I won't, because there will be only a few hundred people who will ever want to purchase it. I'd probably do better by playing the lotto!

No, instead, I am happy you've purchased it because it probably means you've made the commitment to a career of helping people improve their chances for good health or medical outcomes.

Those people may be patients diagnosed with a difficult disease - or happily pregnant women who want birthing assistance. They may be young children - or older, fragile elders. They may already be quite healthy and want to stay that way – or they may be out-of-shape, overweight smokers who need someone to coach them to improved health.

You are available to hold their hands, educate them, manage their expectations, calm them, remove some of their fear and in general – yes – advocate for them.

You are my hero. And I love that one of my heroes has purchased my book!

Why I Wrote This Book

In 2004, I had a horrific run-in with the healthcare system. I was diagnosed with a rare, terminal form of lymphoma and given only a few months to live. Over the next several months, I figured out on my own that the diagnosis was wrong. After some campaigning and lobbying with a second opinion oncologist, the biopsy that had precipitated the diagnosis was sent to the National Institutes of Health for confirmation. Their conclusion: no cancer.

My story is well documented in a variety of places[1], but the bottom line was this: I learned that getting decent healthcare isn't easy. From money, to providers who don't stay current, to an insurance system that wants to cut corners, to medical errors and infections, too many hurdles stand in a patient's way of getting the good healthcare he or she needs – the care he or she deserves.

---

1 http://patients.about.com/od/misdiagnosis/a/misdiagnosis.htm

For the 20 years prior to my misdiagnosis odyssey, I had enjoyed a successful marketing career. I had provided marketing services for small businesses, large organizations, and professionals like lawyers, authors and CPAs. Beginning in 1999, I had begun to move my practice into a web-focused specialty, coupled with public relations. By 2001, I had ventured into my own business as a marketing consultant and during the next few years had successfully moved more than 100 businesses to the web where their outreach and success was multiplying.

My clients were happy, I loved my work. I was making a good living. Life was good!

But that misdiagnosis was a major brick wall, and I had run into it head-on. It cost me my trust and all my savings. It knocked me on my keister in a big way, and it wasn't easy to pick myself up.

As I struggled to my feet, trying to recover from the emotional and physical insult such an experience inflicts, I made up my mind I would do three things:

- Warn others about the dysfunctional operation of the healthcare system

- Provide them with the knowledge and tools they would need to get the healthcare they deserve

- Help others advocate for patients who could not otherwise get that good care

And so I have. Beginning in early 2005, I branded myself as Every Patient's Advocate, and began writing and speaking on topics that would further my goals. Today I have a long list of activities that help me accomplish my mission of helping people get improved healthcare, no matter what their circumstances.

One such activity is a website called AdvoConnection.com[2]. It's a service that allows patients or their caregivers to search a directory of health advocates, find the help they need, and make contact with the people they think are most likely to provide the services they need.

Driving the public advocate search site is the an organization called the Alliance of Professional Health Advocates[2] where all forms of health-related advocates can find business support.

Of course, one of the biggest areas of support is – you guessed it – marketing. It's support that is needed by all members, and it's the aspect of an advocate's business for which I can provide the most help.

Your Need for Marketing Knowledge and Assistance

Marketing isn't rocket science. In fact, it can be one of the most fulfilling, fun and measurable aspects of your advocacy business. Once you get the hang of branding, target

---

2 http://APHAdvocates.org

audiences, networking and outreach, you'll find yourself thinking in terms of marketing as a constant backdrop to all the work you do.

This book is the tool that will help you get there. You'll feel accomplished, your business will grow, and your goals – and mine – will be met.

Thank you for inviting my advice into your knowledge bank. I am confident you'll find it useful. I look forward to your great success, helping as many people as possible get the great healthcare they deserve.

How to Use This Book

This book is called a handbook, because it's intended to help you do three things:

1. **Develop a basic understanding of marketing** as it applies to a service such as health advocacy.

2. Based on your new knowledge, **build a marketing plan** as a useful and integral part of your overall business plan.

3. **Implement the strategies and tactics** you've defined yourself through use of this handbook to build a successful (or more successful) business.

It all sounds so simple, doesn't it?

Truth is, understanding and implementing marketing doesn't have to be difficult or expensive, regardless of what you may think. Like anything else, you will need to develop your expertise one step at a time. But I promise you that once you've read just the first few chapters of this handbook, you'll begin thinking about your business very differently from the way you've thought about it before.

The key is to maximize what you can get from this book. To help you do so, I recommend you do the following:

Glance through the whole book first. You don't need to get into the nitty gritty yet. Just get an overview of what we're going to cover:

1. Strategy

2. Then tools and tactics

3. THEN goal setting and building your marketing plan

4. Finally, assessing how much of your time and money it will require to implement

Then **read the book more carefully, performing the tasks** that are assigned with each section.

IMPORTANT! Print out the free workbook that goes along with this book. It organizes all your tasks for building your marketing plan and has little hints that aren't included in this book to make them easier to do. Since you purchased this handbook, there's no additional charge for printing the workbook.

Find it at: http://HealthAdvocateResources.com/HABMH

Find resources in Chapter Sixteen. I've provided additional resources for much of the information and many of the tasks mentioned in this book – and more.

Understand that your plan and implementation will both EVOLVE. You don't write them down, then ignore them or expect they will happen over time. You may want to return to this handbook on occasion – a point we'll make again in Chapter Fifteen.

Most books of this type begin by asking you to set goals – in this case, marketing goals. Don't roll your eyes! Just to show you how different this book is, we aren't going to try to set any goals until we have a better idea of what goals we can set at all. By the time you get to that part, it should be easier.

That's all you need to know about getting the most from this handbook, so let's get started....

Chapter One
Marketing Basics: Strategy, Tactics and Planning for Success

Marketing is the most important tool any business owner has.

OK – I realize your lawyer and CPA told you the same thing about their services. But I believe it's true. Without effective marketing, you won't have new clients, nor will your business grow, and eventually, you will no longer be in business. That's only partially true for your lawyer and your CPA.

What exactly do I mean by marketing? A quick definition: effective marketing is learning what goods and services your potential clients need, then making sure they know you are available to fulfill those needs. It's the education component of business – teaching potential buyers that you are ready and able to help them out.

The Dreaded Task: Building a Marketing Plan

As you've researched starting a business, or even worked with one of the business-support services like the Small Business Administration, you've been encouraged to build a business plan. Among other activities, your business plan has helped you set your goals, frame your business structure, even anticipate your budget and cash flow.

Of course, a huge component of your business plan is your marketing plan. Marketing is one of the largest and most worthwhile investments you'll make, not just as you start up your business, but as it develops and grows.

Many people get stuck developing their marketing plans because they just don't understand how to do it. I suspect that's why you bought this book – because you recognize that there is much more to it than filling in an outline, then creating a brochure and a website.

Further, it's not good enough to simply develop a marketing plan. No – what we really need is a marketing plan that we actually understand, and even more so, that actually works!

Building a marketing plan is not an easy task. There's background work, development of strategy, creation of tactics and more. Daunting if you don't understand what it all means or how it all fits together.

Strategic Planning vs. Tactical Planning

It's easy for those who haven't been in the marketing trenches for a long time to mix up strategy and tactics. A good marketing plan not only breaks them out, but shows how they will support each other.

Instead of making you wade through a college level course in marketing, I'm going to provide you with a fairly easy way to look at the difference:

Strategic Planning is your big picture, goal-oriented planning. It's the over-arching, big picture planning which will help you define the actual tactics you decide to use. Your branding, messages, target audiences – all those aspects that actually represent how you want your public to recognize you are part of your strategic planning.

Tactical Planning defines the tools that will help you execute and showcase your strategies. Tactics are often framed by the activities we use to make them happen. You'll recognize their names: advertising, public relations, websites, brochures – these are all tools we can use to execute the tactical part of a marketing plan. So, for example, you might decide to develop a brochure to distribute to church groups (which will help you increase your client roster), or create a You Tube video aimed at pregnant moms, or place an ad in the newspaper in another city (which helps you expand your geography). Tactics help you accomplish the goals you set forth in your strategic planning.

Not so difficult to understand, right? Now that you better understand the basic differences, let me explain how we'll use that knowledge to create your marketing plan.

How This Book Will Help You Build Your Effective Marketing Plan

A marketing plan done right will be a roadmap – a tool that will provide a clarity about your business you didn't have before, and an approach to your work that makes far more sense than it ever did.

So that's what this book will do for you – provide the background and framework to help you develop that plan that works for you. Here's how:

We'll begin the book with discussions about **strategy** – people, benefits, messages, branding and more. As you better understand each step, you'll take notes for your own plan.

Once you understand strategy, we'll look at **tactics** – your choices of tools you may use to execute your strategy – from use of the Web to public relations and collateral materials – how you can use them to market your business. This book will help you apply your strategy, using the right tactics for your business.

As we go through each step, you'll find some sidebars of information that add to your knowledge – some reinforcement ideas or challenges to your thinking.

Many steps will have assignments for you – you'll see them identified as **TASKS**. If you take the time to perform those tasks, the result will be the basis for your own business marketing plan. In other words, just following along may help you complete that dreaded marketing plan development you've avoided until now!

Marketing Is Not the Same As Sales

Earlier in this chapter, I provided a definition of marketing as making sure potential clients or buyers know you are able to provide the goods or services they need.

Please notice that I didn't say your potential clients will "purchase your services" or "buy what you're selling." Those are actually sales activities.

- Marketing is about creating demand.
- Sales is about satisfying that demand. Sales can't and won't happen without marketing.

In larger organizations and big corporations, sales and marketing obviously work closely together, but they are often performed by different departments.

But if you are a one-person company or run a small business with only a few advocates, then you'll find your marketing and sales are pretty much the same thing performed by the same person, or at least overseen by the same person. You, perhaps together with a marketing consultant, will develop the marketing strategy and tactics you, yourself will use, to sell your services.

All this to explain that your marketing plan is not a field of dreams… just because you build it doesn't mean your clients will come to your business.

So I'll provide this reminder here: that building your marketing plan will help you make your sales, but you'll want to be sure it's a tool you can really use so it doesn't just set on a shelf somewhere when you're finished. (I'll provide this caveat at the end of the book, too – just to remind you!)

Next Steps

Discussions of strategy and tactics are really just a lot of marketing-speak that barely recognizes the real heart of all marketing, especially marketing for health-related advocacy businesses.

That heart is people.

So that's where we'll begin our understanding of how marketing strategy works.

Chapter Two
Strategy: People, Problems and Point-of-View

There is no business more personal than health-related business.

Think about this in your own life: As individuals, we perform health or medical-related tasks every day, ranging from preventive choices like brushing our teeth to making food choices (which may or may not be healthy.) We pay insurance premiums and/or taxes to the government who will help us take care of our health. We look both ways before we cross the street, and we pray for friends or relatives who may have health issues. Etcetera....

Now think about this in someone else's life: When they have a health challenge, they may need someone else's help, either to take care of their body (there's nothing more personal than our own bodies) or to take care of their money (perhaps the second most personal thing we have.) As an advocate, that's the role you fulfill.

Duh! You say... this is no surprise. As an advocate, as you actually perform your advocacy work one-on-one with a patient or caregiver, no doubt that's exactly how you treat it – with a very personal, caring, invested-in-positive-outcomes approach. That's *why* you are successful doing your advocacy work.

Now let's switch gears to marketing. Do you also use that same very personal approach in your marketing? You should.

That's what we'll explore in this chapter – understanding people and using that understanding as part of our marketing strategy.

Point of View – An Important Tool

The most effective marketing takes into account the point of view (POV) of the person it is aimed at. Further, it is presented using that point of view.

Point of view is determined by walking in someone else's shoes – seeing the world through his or her lens. In order to understand someone's point of view, you need to understand their hopes and fears, hurdles and frustrations, and what can possibly solve those problems for them – or at least what they THINK will solve them.

This is best represented using an example so you can see how various points of view influence an outcome:

Meet Mrs. Franklin

Mrs. Franklin is 84 and lives alone. She lost her husband six years ago, and her health and cognition have declined ever since. Further, she has some heart problems, and doesn't always remember to take her medicine. She is adamant that she wants to stay in the home she has lived in for almost 40 years, but she knows she needs some help.

Mrs. Franklin, her children and friends; each has a different point of view about her circumstances:

Mrs. Franklin	Is fearful because she is not able to cope with her situation. She wants someone to make the fear go away and she wants to stay at home, in her familiar neighborhood, with her friends nearby.

• • • • • • • • • • • • •

James Franklin, her oldest child	James lives 500 miles away and leads a busy life with his work, his family and his hobbies. He loves his mother and has a good relationship with her. He recognizes that his mother is having problems that he can't help her with from a long distance.

He hopes to find a solution for caring for his mother that doesn't impact his lifestyle any more than it has to. He realizes her preference is to stay in her home, but so far sees no way that can happen.

He also knows it will be expensive for his mother to live in a nursing home. Further, her only asset is her home, and he knows it will need to be sold to have enough money for her to live nearby.

Of course, he has considered letting her move in with his wife and children, but no one can be home during the day to take care of her. Still, that's the least expensive of the options and most convenient to him.

• • • • • • • • • • • • •

Mrs. Franklin's other three children	There is some dissention among James' siblings about how to take care of their mother. Two question James' motive for moving his mother closer to him. None of them have offered workable solutions. When it comes to the idea of selling their mother's home, they just don't agree at all, because one hopes to inherit some money while others recognize that her assets are needed to help pay for her extended care.

Mrs. Franklin's doctor	Realizes that Mrs. Franklin can't take care of herself. He recommends Mrs. Franklin find someone to provide in-home services so she will not be alone but can stay at home. He would very much like Mrs. Franklin to stay in the area because he doesn't want to lose her as a patient.

• • • • • • • • • • • • • •

Mrs. Franklin's health insurer	As an American citizen, Mrs. Franklin is covered by Medicare. She also has a Medicare Advantage program that covers some of her other needs. She does not have long-term care insurance. Her Advantage insurer may not cover her needs in a nursing home unless it's located in the state in which she pays her premiums.

• • • • • • • • • • • • • •

Mrs. Franklin's neighbors	The neighbors have been pitching in to keep Mrs. Franklin's lawn cut, her driveway plowed and taking her mail in from the street. They know she needs more assistance and don't really understand why her kids aren't doing more to help her.

• • • • • • • • • • • • • •

Mrs. Franklin's pastor	Mrs. Franklin was always very active in her church. She sang in the choir, taught Sunday School for many years, and her church donations total well over $10,000 each year. Her pastor hopes James won't move his mother to another location because he can't afford for her annual donations to stop. Plus, they've had several discussions over the years about how she would like her funeral to be arranged and where she would like to be buried.

• • • • • • • • • • • • • •

Mrs. Franklin's friends	Mrs. Franklin still gets to her bridge club once a week, although last week she got lost driving to the hostess's home (yes – she's still driving!) They know she needs additional help, and two of them know her children. One has decided to contact James to talk to him about assistance for his mother.

One woman, one situation, but many points of view. Each of these people will be affected by whatever decisions are made by Mrs. Franklin or on Mrs. Franklin's behalf. Further, each has an idea of what they do, or don't, think should happen to Mrs. Franklin.

Of course, not all these people would hire you for your advocacy services. But each one could have an influence on whether you get hired. A good marketing plan will account for various points of view, and will use those points of view strategically and tactically.

From potential clients, to caregivers, to those who have an influence on the choice of an advocate, to other advocates, our competitors and the media, there are many people who can hire us, help us, stand in our way – or all three. These people comprise our "target audiences" and we need to include their points of view into our marketing plans.

▲

B to B? or B to C?

Here's some marketing-speak for you. (Use it to impress business friends?)

You'll hear marketers refer to "B-to-B" or "B-to-C". Here's what they mean:

B-to-B refers to business-to-business. When your business provides goods or services to other businesses, then you use a B-to-B marketing model. For example, if you target your support services to other advocacy businesses, or you are hired by a business owner to assist his employees, your model would be considered B-to-B even though your services are still focused on an individual.

B-to-C refers to business-to-consumer. If your primary clients or customers are individuals (consumers) then your business is considered B-to-C. For example, if the child of an elderly parent hires you, or an individual hires you directly to help review his hospital bill then your marketing model is B-to-C.

Some businesses use both models. As a private advocate, you may have one contract with an employer to be on call with employees (B-to-B), or you may be hired directly by someone to help them transition through an illness B-to-C).

The only reason this is important is to help you define and then market to your target audiences. Use the distinction between the two models to help you develop your marketing messages (See Chapter Three).

▼

Target Audience #1: People Who Will Hire Us

Who actually hires you as an advocate or coach? Those answers will vary depending on what type of business you have, but we can make some generalizations.

Patients are a good start for most of us because they know they need an advocate or coach to fix something that isn't right for them – not in the medical sense (because they'll rely on doctors and other providers for that). Rather, to fix their confusion, frustration, wallets – some other aspect of obtaining or affording healthcare that just isn't the way they want it to be.

But sometimes the person who will hire us isn't the person who actually needs the help. Just like Mrs. Franklin's case, sometimes the child of an elderly person will recognize that help is needed. Or a parent of a young child born with a disability will feel like he or she needs assistance. Or a pregnant woman's husband, or the spouse of a patient recently released from the hospital is overwhelmed by the hospital's bill.

Yes -- There may be a difference between the people we do our work for, and the people who pay us to do that work. Not only that, there may be a difference in their goals. And sometimes their goals will conflict with each other. Remember – it's all about their points of view.

Effective marketing takes into account the many different people who may hire us and what their motivations might be.

Depending on your business model, here are some people who might possibly hire you:

- A patient who is sick and needs assistance (B to C)

- A patient who is not as healthy as he or she might wish (applicable for a health coach) (B to C)

TASK #1

Make a list of the people who might hire you – the ones who will actually write you a check or give you a credit card number to do your work for them or someone they care about. Add notes about their points of view.

....

A reminder that you can download the free companion workbook to The Health Advocate's Marketing Handbook from http://HealthAdvocateResources.com/HABMH

- A pregnant woman who needs birthing help or a lactation coach (B to C)

- A recently released patient who needs help reviewing hospital bills (B to C)

- A patient who needs home health care (B to C)

- A patient's spouse, partner, child or other relative – for any of the goals listed previously, or for their own goals, which may conflict (May be B to C or B to B)

Chances are you listed the obvious ones – like the list I provided to you on the last page. But now it's time to expand your thought process. There may be others who will hire you that you haven't thought of before. Again, it's best to show some examples of how to expand your list of people who might hire you:

- A medical/navigational advocate could be hired by a concierge or boutique doctor who would see the advocate's assistance as a great way to save money for his or her practice. (B to B)

- A home health advocate might be hired by an attorney for an elderly person who didn't have relatives who could step in to help. (B to B)

- A health coach might be hired by a business owner or HR department of a company that wished to improve the health of its employees. (B to B)

TASK #2

Return to your list and add some new possibilities along with their points of view. As you continue reading this book, you may be able to add more.

....

A reminder that you can download the free companion workbook to The Health Advocate's Marketing Handbook from http://HealthAdvocateResources.com/HABMH

Now you have a better understanding of who your actual clients can be, and a good sense of the strategy needed for defining who they are and why they might hire you.

Clients are your primary target audience.

There are two other types, but they are **secondary target audiences**, removed from the actual hiring and paying process, but still very important.

Target Audience #2: People Who Can Help Us Get Hired - Influencers

There are many people who may not hire us directly, but might influence someone else to hire us.

Some are obvious. For example, a grandparent-to-be might encourage her daughter to hire an advocate to help out during a pregnancy. Or a happy client – say one for whom a billing advocacy company found a $20 thousand discrepancy in her hospital billing – may talk to others about her positive experience with that advocate.

But others may not be as obvious. A rabbi might have read about your services in the local paper and may suggest a family contact you. You don't have a direct relationship with the rabbi, yet the rabbi influenced the contact. The family he made the recommendation to trusts him and based on what he heard about you, he somehow trusts that you can help.

Media as Influencers

One huge audience is the media. Media includes print (newspapers, magazines), TV (local broadcast, or cable), radio (local broadcast, internet or satellite), and properties on the Internet such as Internet radio shows, blogs and social media.

The reason media is such an important group of influencers is because they can help educate large audiences and hopefully, steer them towards you.

Later in this book, in Chapter Eight (Public Relations), we'll take a closer look at media.

Or maybe you'll give a talk at a local senior center. When one of the attendee's friends must be hospitalized, the senior who attended your talk may suggest the friend get in touch with you to be her bedside advocate.

What makes someone an influencer? They are people who are trusted and respected by others, enough so that their recommendations are given some weight by the people who will hire you.

There may be dozens of influencers who can be useful to you – part of your marketing strategy should be helping them understand what your services are and why you are a good choice for hiring, then making sure they refer potential clients to you when the time comes.

Here are some obvious influencers:

- Friends of the patient

- Neighbors

- Clergy

- Fellow club members: think everything from the Elks and Moose to the VFW and the country club

- Doctors and other healthcare workers

- Former clients – patients or their loved ones who you have worked for before and are so grateful they will say nice things

Here are some less obvious influencers:

- Lawyers, CPAs and financial advisors, especially those who work in eldercare or with worker's compensation

- Pharmacists, especially those who run neighborhood pharmacies and get to know their customers and their customers' needs

- Other personal service workers like hairdressers and barbers

- Media – newspaper reporters, news anchors, bloggers

- Other advocates who perform different, but complementary services to yours

- Other advocates who do the same work as you, but in a different geographical region

Overall, their interest may not be directly about the potential client or patient. It may be more about feeling good that they were able to help solve a problem – the problem that needs a professional – you – to solve it. Even still, it's great strategy to influence some of these people to tell others about your services. Word of mouth is extremely powerful.

TASK #3

Make a list of influencers for your advocacy business, along with who they may be able to influence. Include the points of view of those influencers.

....

A reminder that you can download the free companion workbook to
The Health Advocate's Marketing Handbook from
http://HealthAdvocateResources.com/HABMH

Target Audience #3: People Who Can Stand In Our Way (But Might Not)

Not everyone will be predisposed to recommend our services to someone else. Word of mouth can be powerfully positive or damagingly negative.

There are three categories of people who might not want to recommend us, and not only can they stand in the way of our being hired by a potential client, but they might sully our reputations, too. They are:

- Our competitors

- Friends and associates of our competitors

- Clients or their friends and loved ones who have not been happy with our work in the past

But many businesses have shifted attitudes about competition over the past decade. In fact, a new word really describes it well. That is "**coopetition**" -- yes – a combination of cooperation and competition.

The concept of **coopetition** is based on the recognition that there is plenty of business out there, and that helping each other means we help ourselves.

Again, let's look at an example:

Joe Smith has been a health coach for almost 8 years. He calls himself Joe the Health Coach, and he is well-recognized in his community as Joe the Health Coach.

Fran Jones is also a health coach, located in the next block from Joe. She's much newer in the business of coaching, and is not nearly so well recognized.

Show Me the Money

Is every patient or caregiver a potential client?

A short answer – no. And the distinction has nothing to do with a diagnosis, or a hospital bill or a pregnancy or a need to lose weight. The answer has to do with whether the patient (or the person hiring you) can afford to pay you for your work.

Most advocates, and that probably includes you, have big hearts. As a big-hearted person, it's tempting to want to work for everyone who asks you for help. In particular, early in your career, it will be tempting to take on clients without charging them for your services or by discounting your pricing so they can afford to hire you.

It may make sense early in your career to take on cases that won't pay you much, in order to gain some experience and build your resumé. But be wary of taking on pro bono work that will require you to spend time you could spend on marketing, or even better, on working with a paying client. If you work on a percentage basis (e.g. taking a percent of the amount you save someone on their hospital bill) be sure you will get paid before someone bankrupts or just skips out on the bill.

As an advocate in business, your focus needs to be on keeping yourself in business. If you win the lottery one day, you can take on all that pro bono work. But for now, better to concentrate on building your clientele and reputation.

On the face of it, and if you took a look at their business cards or their yellow pages ads, you would think Fran and Joe are competitors, right?

But it turns out, they aren't really business competitors at all. Fran specializes in helping women, particularly those who have weathered difficult treatment regimens like surgery or breast cancer.

Joe, on the other hand, is a fitness guy. He is a health food nazi, a strength trainer and teaches boxing.

Fran and Joe can be coopetition because even though they are both health coaches, they have different target markets. They definitely need to talk to each other, and they can possibly refer clients to each other.

That form of coopetition is easy to understand. But suppose you do exactly the same work another advocate does in the same area?

In some cases it just helps to remain friendly. That can be your entire strategy – remain friendly. Never speak negatively about the other, never tell tales that you wouldn't want being told about you.

But in other cases, it helps to refer clients to each other. You may get too busy to handle a project for a patient (too many pregnant women needing your midwife or doula services at the same time, for example) – so be the very helpful person and refer a potential client to your competitor. The next time your competitor gets too busy, she may refer an extra client to you.

Another way to see the difference is like this: Being competitors is a passive relationship. Because both of you run the same kind of business you are, by definition, competitors.

On the other hand, being each other's coopetition is an active relationship. You will each work at helping the other in order to help both your businesses. You become each other's influencers.

TASK #4

List your competitors and their likelihood of being your coopetition (influencers) for you. What is the benefit to them to providing that influence? (That's their point of view.)

....

A reminder that you can download the free companion workbook to
The Health Advocate's Marketing Handbook from
http://HealthAdvocateResources.com/HABMH

There is a particular reason why such coopetition is important for health advocates. That is, that most people don't yet understand what a health advocate is, or does, or how that advocate can help them. In order for the general public to gain this understanding, we must all be in education mode – beyond marketing only our own company's services and capabilities, we are educating the public about the existence and benefits of working with advocates, too. By being cooperative with someone who does the work you do, the education component of advocacy will be maximized.

Further, friends and colleagues of your competitors can be influenced positively by your coopetition. They may end up being your friends and colleagues, too.

Now that we understand how each target audience plays a role in our success, and how to walk in their shoes to determine their points of view, let's look at the next step in determining our strategies; that is, figuring out how to help them see that we can help solve their problems.

Chapter Three
Strategy: Benefits, Messages and Expectations

With a better understanding of the people involved in our marketing – our target audiences – it's time to develop our strategy for making sure they understand how we can help them. We'll do that through development of specific marketing messages. Those messages will be framed using the points of view of our target audiences.

(That's a lot of marketing-speak, don't you think? But I'm betting you understood it. Told you it's not all that difficult....)

We'll begin with two tasks that will help you define your business:

TASK #5

Make a master list of the services you offer to any client who might hire you. Your list might include activities such as:

- Accompany patients to doctor's appointments
- Sit at the patient's bedside in the hospital
- Research medical information
- Pre- and post-partum assistance
- Teach Lamaze or La Leche methods
- Review hospital bills for discrepancies
- Negotiate with insurers to get permissions or overcome care denials
- Help families choose a nursing home for an elderly loved one

....

A reminder that you can download the free companion workbook to
The Health Advocate's Marketing Handbook from
http://HealthAdvocateResources.com/HABMH

TASK #6

Describe your expertise. What makes you (or your staff) the right person to do this work for a potential customer or client? What specific education, skills and experience do you have that makes you the person who should be hired to be an advocate?

Include attributes like how many years of experience you have, the fact that you are conveniently located (if you are), well-organized, have satisfied clients, or anything else you think is important for your prospective clients to know specifically about you, such as:

- We have three nurses on staff with almost 100 years experience among us.
- We have 10 years of experience negotiating hospital bills and have saved our clients more than $1 million.
- I have attended more than 100 births, delivering 107 babies, all healthy.

....

A reminder that you can download the free companion workbook to
The Health Advocate's Marketing Handbook from
http://HealthAdvocateResources.com/HABMH

Once you're finished with your lists, set them aside. We'll refer to them again shortly.

Why Do People Want or Need to Hire an Advocate?

Why does anyone need any product or service? Let's look at the answer to this question through your own experience, asking:

Why did you buy the last pair of shoes you bought?

Maybe you bought them because you loved the way they looked, or because they went with your new outfit. Maybe they are functional and you had worn out your last pair. Or maybe you bought shoes for someone else – your child – who needed them for school.

People pay good money for things because they have a motivation to do so. That motivation ranges from wanting something for the sake of wanting it, to needing something for the sake of real, death-defying need.

It's that motivation that the best marketers tap into – and use – to compel people to purchase their products and services.

If you were selling new cars (a fun new product), or you were a golf pro (teaching people how to improve their games or play a new sport), then I'd be encouraging you to look at your business and your marketing very differently. Those are products and services that people WANT, but they don't necessarily need.

As a health advocate, you provide a service people NEED instead of want. At least people perceive they need your assistance. Since they are dealing with health or money issues, they are afraid of what they will lose if they don't tap into your services. That's a simple point to understand if you arehelping people get decent healthcare, or if you are trying to help someone save thousands on their hospital bills.

But that point is even true for most health coaches or midwives or geriatric care or palliative care professionals. Why do most people want to lose weight or get into better shape? Because they either want to look better, or live longer or healthier, or both. Why do women want assistance with giving birth? Because they don't like the approach being used in hospitals, and they perceive their delivery process will be healthier for their babies and themselves. Why does an adult child seek help for an older parent who is close to death? People die every day without assistance. But the person who hires someone to assist a dying patient wishes to make that process as pain-free and peaceful as possible.

The FUDGE Theory

Professional marketers sometimes refer to a theory called **FUD**, which stands for Fear, Uncertainty and Doubt. The great majority of your primary target audiences, those clients who will specifically hire you and pay you, are fearful, uncertain or doubtful about their outcomes. They feel like their lives are out of control. They need you and hope you'll be

Managing Expectations

You'll find the concept of managing expectations throughout this book, but we'll begin here, where we are talking about your potential clients and their point of view.

For many, healthcare feels like it's a right, not a privilege. Indeed, if you live and work in Canada, basic healthcare IS a right. But that's not true in the United States. Most people just think it is.

Along with that perception of healthcare being a right, many people have thought it was "free" or close to free. They may be Medicare or Medicaid recipients who have paid little or nothing – or weren't aware that they did pay for many years through their paychecks when they were younger, for the services that they receive today.

As a result, sometimes people have very unrealistic expectations of those they ask for help from. They may feel entitled to certain services or advice. They may feel insulted when you tell them they must pay you for your work. Or they may think that once they pay you anything at all, you owe them the moon, plus an extra star or two.

Early in your communication, long before you actually sign a contract with them, make sure you and your potential client understand exactly the same things. Don't let them have one set of expectations while you have another. Don't assume they understand your work, or let them think you can provide a service you can't provide. Be very clear about what you can't do, and what you can do, in what time frame, for what amount of money.

The better you manage their expectations, the less you'll have to deal with that sense of entitlement, and the more successful your relationship and outcomes will be.

able to remove their fear, uncertainty and doubt.

Experienced advocates have identified additional motivations on the parts of potential clients. In fact, they have added to FUD to call it **FUDGE**. Fear, Uncertainty and Doubt—plus GUILT and EXHAUSTION. Guilt, perhaps on the parts of spouses / partners, or adult children who feel as if they must support their debilitated spouse or partner, or elderly Mom or Dad not because they want to, but because they will feel guilty if they don't. Then there are caregivers who are exhausted, perhaps juggling elderly parents, children at home, a full time job, and just feel as if they can't keep up—recognizing that an advocate could help them reclaim some quality to their lives.

Other professionals call these attributes "pains". They describe pain very broadly. A patient's "pain" can be frustration that the doctor is always running an hour late. Or it might be that he has just been told he needs yet another test. Or his pain can be his most recent hospital bill that seems exorbitant and unfair.

Regardless of what we call it – FUDGE, or pain, or anything else – the reason someone might want to hire you is to fix something they think is wrong. Further, they have an expectation that if they hire you, you WILL fix what is wrong. That's their point of view. They believe that once you fix it, the fear, uncertainty and doubt will be relieved. They'll feel much better.

They expect you will deliver peace-of-mind.

Your Prospective Clients' Lens

Our prospective clients aren't doing this analysis of why they need an advocate. They don't know anything about motivators or marketing theory, any more than you did before you began reading this chapter. They just feel in their hearts and heads that they need help.

Interestingly, having only that basic feeling of the fact that they need help, most of them will approach their search for that help in exactly the same way, using the same steps:

Step One: People will identify their pain and need.

For example: "I am so scared about my new diagnosis, I need someone to help me figure out what to do." Or, "The doctor says I'll have another heart attack if I don't lose weight, but I've tried losing weight dozens of times! I need someone to coach me." Or "I hate the entire thought of bringing my baby into such a sterile, uncaring, loud and bright environment. I want to find someone who offers an alternative."

Step Two: They will figure out who or what provides the solution (relieves their pain, provides peace-of-mind).

---

3   Because patient advocacy is so new, many people don't understand that they must pay for these services privately. This is an extra area where advocates must be careful to manage expectations. Coaches, midwives and some other health-related advocates may not have this same hurdle.

The person who is frightened of a diagnosis will go online or will ask friends if they know of someone who can help them sort out their options and fears. The guy who had the heart attack will start calling about the prices of gyms and oh, by the way, do they have someone who can coach him? The woman who wants a more peaceful birth for her baby will begin exploring potential doulas and midwives online, too – and she'll ask her friends if they

Educating Our Audiences

Marketers and business people love graphs! And one graph you'll often find in a marketing text book is one that shows the lifecycle of a product. A basic one looks like this:

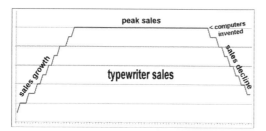

Typewriter sales were fairly slow when they were first invented, but then sales climbed. When computers came long, sales began to fall. Today, few typewriters are sold compared to their peak.

This graph is easiest understood for a new product. Take typewriters, for example. The first many years after typewriters were invented, people were slow to adopt them. Then once they became more affordable and people understand how to use them, typewriter sales increased exponentially. Of course, once the 1980s rolled around, sales of typewriters began to decline. Today, few are sold at all.

In those early typewriter years, manufacturers had to do some educating about what typewriters were for, and help people and businesses understand how their work would improve if they purchased typewriters. Once they got past that hurdle, sales soared.

As advocates, we are faced with a similar challenge in these, our early years. Most of our potential clients have no idea we exist, nor how their lives will improve if they hire us. We will hit our stride within a few years. (One goal, of course, is to make sure our graph never takes a dive like the one for typewriters does.)

To ensure the growth of advocacy in these early years, some of our messaging needs to be educational in nature. It's not enough just to say, "Hi, I'm a patient advocate!" That needs to be accompanied by some education which will include what kinds of services you can provide, the fact that you charge a fee or require a contract to do so, and managing what someone's expectations can be from the process.

Efforts are underway through the Alliance of Professional Health Advocates to provide materials and opportunities to do this educating.

Further efforts are underway to develop a nationally or internationally recognized credential for health advocates to ensure some consistency among skill sets. If you would like to know more about these efforts, sign up for notices at this book's website, found in Chapter Sixteen's Resources.

know of someone who can fill that roll.

Step Three: After identifying a potential solution, they determine whether the solution is accessible or whether it creates a hurdle.

Accessibility means three things: geography, time and cost.

If what they need requires you to be nearby, they will look for that. If you are nearby, they'll email or pick up the phone.

If you have your charges listed in your brochure or on your website, they will look at that, too. If they think your services are worth that much money, then they will contact you. If they think that's too expensive, they won't.[3] If you don't list your charges anywhere, they may make an assumption that is true, or untrue. Maybe they will call or email to find out what your charge, or maybe they won't.

The only determination left will be whether you are truly available to help them, and this is often something that doesn't occur to them unless you bring it up. You will have to determine for each potential client whether you have time in your schedule to take them on. They may ask the question[4], but if they don't, you'll want to be sure to raise it for them.

Remember that for all three of these steps, it's their perception that is important, and not the reality of the situation. Someone who just got a huge hospital bill may think they need someone who is nearby – or even in the same state they live in – to handle it for them, even if that's not true. Someone who acquired an infection in a hospital may believe they can sue the hospital for all it's worth, but that may not be true either.

As we develop our marketing messages, we need to address these perceptions and misperceptions, taking into account that sometimes the potential client doesn't really understand what she really needs or what kind of assistance is available to help her.

Services Morph to Benefits

Now let's take the list of services you created and edit them to what we know about that desire for peace of mind, improved health, saved money – any positive outcome that evolves from the services you provide. In effect, we are morphing your list of services— things you do -- to a list of benefits - pain relief and peace of mind -- to your potential clients.

Benefits are much more personal than a list of services, but they shouldn't replace that list. They will be used hand in hand. When your list of services is combined with your list of benefits, then you have a good start on development of your marketing messages.

---

4   People looking for an advocate may access a suggested list of interview questions to ask you
     when they are determining whether you are the right person to help them. Find the questions here:
     http://advoconnection.com/chooseanadvocate.htm

TASK #7

Rewrite your list of services into a list of benefits with both peace of mind, and the client's point of view as their basis.

....

A reminder that you can download the free companion workbook to
The Health Advocate's Marketing Handbook from
http://HealthAdvocateResources.com/HABMH

Further, defining your benefits allows you to introduce additional plusses to working with you that defining services doesn't provide. For example, maybe your location is a benefit, even though it's not really a service.

Include some benefits that reflect your expertise, too.

Examples:

- We offer peace of mind as we sit by your hospital bedside and monitor your care.
- We offer the peace of mind you'll get from knowing someone can reduce your hospital bills by negotiating them on your behalf.
- Your baby's birth will be far more peaceful with a doula by your side.
- We are located nearby in Yourtown, USA – OR – we work with clients across the country.
- You'll rest easier knowing you can potentially save thousands of dollars.
- Our 30 years of nursing experience ensures you that we know how to talk to the doctors and get their attention.

Developing Your Marketing Messages

Now let's take the list of services and benefits you created and edit them to what we know about that desire for peace of mind, improved health, saved money and more. These will be your marketing messages, and you'll need them as you create your marketing tactics for your marketing plan.

You've already done the hard work, making a master list of services and benefits, and defining your expertise. Shifting these into marketing messages is actually quite easy because your marketing messages are just a subset of these first two lists.

Don't forget to keep FUDGE—that concept of fear, uncertainty, doubt, guilt and exhaustion—in your mind. While not all messages need to be focused on those ideas, for health advocates they will, necessarily, play a large role.

Services Messages – Begin your list of marketing messages with your list of services. Condense them into categories, and edit them so they don't ramble.

Example:

Your services list includes such activities as health assessments, medical appointment accompaniment, diagnosis research, insurance review, hospital bedside monitoring and drug reviews. These are great services, and should all be listed, but they can be presented in a more orderly fashion, grouped and organized.

XYZ Advocates:

- Develops health assessments, including review of all the patient's drugs for potential conflicts.

- Accompanies patients to medical appointments, or sit by their hospital bedside to monitor care.

Benefits Messages – These will require some massaging. The key is to make them sound like they are aimed personally at the reader, and to make the reader come away thinking "that's exactly what I need!"

Example for XYZ Advocates:

- We will develop an assessment of your current health status. Included will be a review of the drugs and supplements you take to be sure drug conflicts are not creating additional health problems for you.

- We will accompany you to medical appointments to help you better understand your provider's information and the answers to your questions. We'll make sure you have the background understanding you need to make informed decisions.

- We will sit by your bedside in the hospital to minimize the chances for problems with your care and help you rest easier and heal properly.

Your Positioning Statement

"Positioning Statement" does sound very marketing, doesn't it? At this point, developing your positioning statement should be a cake-walk – because you've already done the hard part.

A positioning statement is a one sentence (OK, it's a long sentence!) description of exactly what you do, for whom, and why. In fact, it's such a finite sentence that there's a formula you can use to arrive at it.

There's another practically interchangeable term for a positioning statement. Some people call them **elevator speeches or elevator pitches**. The idea is that if someone joins you on an elevator, and asks you what you do for a living, you should be able to answer the question within 12-15 seconds, before they get off the elevator. We'll look at these more closely in Chapter Seven.

Why is a positioning statement important? Because it becomes the simplest description of what you do, or more-so, what your company does, so when anyone asks, you can fire off the answer quickly.

TASK #8

Fill in these blanks to arrive at your positioning statement:

I own/work for/founded _____. We provide _____ (services) to _____ (target audiences) who _____ (why they need your services). Unlike _____ (a competitor or difference, not as effective service), we are able to ensure _____ (target audience) will _____ (their benefit for working with you.)

....

A reminder that you can download the free companion workbook to
The Health Advocate's Marketing Handbook from
http://HealthAdvocateResources.com/HABMH

Here are some examples of how these blanks might be filled by an advocate:

- We provide exercise coaching services to adults who have recently suffered from a heart attack. Unlike trying to handle their exercise plans on their own, we are able to ensure they will stick to their regimens.

- We provide midwifery services to pregnant women who wish to give birth at home with a minimum of medical interference. We are able to ensure excellent prenatal care and safe deliveries.

- We provide hospital bedside monitoring services to patients who must be hospitalized and wish to have an advocate by their sides. Unlike a patient who has only a family member who is not familiar with medical protocols, or perhaps is left alone, we are able to track medications, monitor hand washing and infection control and in general keep the patient safer, ensuring a speedier and more comfortable hospital stay.

TASK #9

Using your services list and your benefits list, develop your marketing messages.

....

A reminder that you can download the free companion workbook to
The Health Advocate's Marketing Handbook from
http://HealthAdvocateResources.com/HABMH

Your USP – Unique Selling Proposition

Here's more marketing-speak for you: USP

Your USP is your Unique Selling Proposition. It's the one thing, among all the services and products you provide, among all the benefits you bring to an advocate-patient relationship, that makes you unique. It's what sets you apart from every other patient advocate in the market – your competitors. It's the bottom line of why someone will actually write you a check for your work.

Think of it this way. McDonalds and Burger King both sell hamburgers. What is unique about either of them? Why would you choose one over the other? You might choose Burger King – because they "uniquely" broil or grill their burgers and maybe that's how you like them cooked. Or you might choose McDonalds because your kids or grandkids like their attached playgrounds. Or you might choose one or the other because of its location. Broiling burgers or offering playgrounds are USPs.

A USP should be related to your services and benefits. It defines what is valuable to your target audience, and what should make you the answer to their fear, uncertainty and doubt.

Use Active Verbs

The best marketing messages use active verbs and second person (referring to "you"), helping your potential client picture you doing those things you say you will do – personally, for them. Here's an example:

> We help people understand their treatment options.
> *(not active, not personal)*

> *vs.*

> We will research your potential treatment options, determine the pros and cons, and explain the differences, so you can decide which option is right for you.
> *(active and personal)*

Words like "research," "determine," "explain" and "decide" – these verbs all replace "understand" and have a much bigger impact on the person reading them.

Note: These active verbs and the second person approach won't work well for your positioning statement, but they work well in most of your marketing messages.

TASK #10

Make an attempt at developing your USP. But don't sweat it right now... you may find it comes easier as we progress in planning.

....

A reminder that you can download the free companion workbook to The Health Advocate's Marketing Handbook from http://HealthAdvocateResources.com/HABMH

Examples:

> XYZ Advocates provides 24/7 care – on call whenever you need us.

> Or

> XYZ Advocates' 30 years of nursing experience can help you overcome your medical challenges.

Refining Your Messages

About this time in the process of developing a marketing plan, most of us feel burned out. Getting through the messaging parts is difficult work, no matter how well you know your business.

At this point, your best bet is to put your messages away, then revisit them in a few days. New ideas and ways to refine them will come to you in the interim. Make notes, then go back and edit them to the extent you feel that's helpful.

Once you've worked on your messages two or three times, then it's time to call in a few folks who can help you. Ideally the people you ask will be people who represent your main target audiences. Don't ask your spouse or even your adult kids or parents – they love you and they aren't objective!

Instead, ask someone who represents your target audience, if you can. Maybe you've done work for someone already who would be willing to review your services, benefits and resulting messages with you? Or perhaps someone who is just like your target audience would spend some time with you (an elderly man across the street, the pregnant mom of one of the other kids on your daughter's soccer team...)

Listen carefully to what they tell you – and listen between the lines, too. They won't be the best at framing their thoughts and feelings because they aren't as invested as you, nor do they probably know much about marketing. So don't worry about wordsmithing. Just worry about concepts and new ideas. You can tweak the actual words and sentences later.

Keywords

Keywords as messages have become more and more important with the advancing use of the Internet for marketing. Since we've just spent so much time reviewing the words we will use in our marketing, now is the best time to think of keywords, too.

Keywords are simply those words your target audiences will use to define and find you. The important words in that sentence are "your target audiences will use" because the words they use aren't necessarily the words we use!

Here's an easy way to understand that. Think of the words doctors use to describe a diagnosis or body function. That's med-speak, and is often confusing to their patients. If someone experiences symptoms, they will look up the symptoms in a search engine – not the actual medical words a doctor might use. THAT is their perspective – their point of view. And we must take the same kind of approach.

An example: without understanding the concept of target audiences, a lactation coach would choose the word "lactation" as a keyword. While that's an important one, a woman who needs help nursing her baby is more likely to use the terms "nursing" or "breast feeding." This coach should list all three among her keywords.

We'll look more closely at keywords in Chapter Ten when it comes time to using them to attract those who search for us on the web.

TASK #11

What keywords represent your services and benefits from your target audiences points of view? Your keywords should include services, benefits, even your geographical location if that's important to your work. Record them now and update them as needed.

....

A reminder that you can download the free companion workbook to
The Health Advocate's Marketing Handbook from
http://HealthAdvocateResources.com/HABMH

Even before you feel as if your messages are finalized for your business, you'll be ready to begin working on your **branding**. That's what we'll tackle in the next chapter.

Chapter Four
Strategy: Developing and Defining Your Brand

We've come a long way since the Circle K.

What's the Circle K and what does it have to do with patient advocacy? Not much at all, actually. But when a non-marketer hears the word "branding" they tend to think of those icons that got burned into the backside of a steer in an old TV western.

In fact, that's where the word "branding" came from. It's the idea of making your business identifiable – to make it clear exactly who you are, what you do, and to distinguish you from other advocates, practically at a glance.

What is Branding?

Branding is simply the representation of your business – in look, in words and in deeds. Many non-marketers think a brand is a logo, like that Circle K, but that's only one aspect of your brand, as we'll understand better in a moment.

There are three components to a brand identity:

- **A graphic look.** This will be your logo, your colors, and maybe even the fonts you use in print materials or the photos you use in a brochure or website.

- **Brand messages.** These are your philosophy and beliefs – and the messages you developed in Chapter Three.

- **An attitude – a personality.** This is a bit tougher to quantify – but your brand's attitude is often a more sub-conscious representation of your company. Some brands are fun (Think Mickey Mouse or Geico.) Others might be heart-warming (like Hallmark.) Another brand might be luxury (Lexus or Nordstroms). An advocate business might want to lean toward trustworthy or comfort-inspiring or life-saving.

Your Brand Makes Promises

When put together, your brand identity creates promises. It's these promises that people think of when they experience your brand:

- When you see a set of golden arches, what do you think of? And if you visit that place, what do they promise you? A hamburger, of course. They also promise you something to satisfy your hunger. AND, they promise you that at any McDonald's in the world, you will get exactly what you expect – a hamburger that tastes like the hamburger at any other McDonalds. When you experience McDonalds, you come away with a sense that golden arches equal hunger satisfaction, fun and consistency.

- How about "We bring good things to life"? GE represents many goods from light bulbs to credit cards (for health purposes) to power-generating turbines. What is their promise? It may be something different for each product they offer, but in general, you have a certain sense of the quality of their goods based on your knowledge and trust of GE. GE's branding is about that trust.

- When I see a rich orange color, I think of Syracuse University. Now – that's because I live near Syracuse, NY. I also think of my college colors (orange and blue) at Bucknell University. But you can probably think of colors that represent your high school or your college, too. Those colors are a part of their brands, as is the animal or other type of mascot that represents them. (Would you believe my high school mascot was a billy goat? Seriously. Williamsville, NY – get it?) For most of us, a school brand promises education, knowledge, friends, memories, networking and nostalgia, too.

The Brand Perception Paradox

The difficult aspect to brand promises is that you will have all the control – and no control. Certainly you can control the graphic representation of a brand and its messages, but you can't control how they are perceived. For example, a vegan looks at McDonald's very differently from the way a six-year-old who loves Happy Meals does. If you live in Florida, you may be a Gators fan who sees that rich orange very differently from the way I do living near Syracuse.

TASK #12:

Begin listing the promises you would like your brand to represent. Those promises will represent concepts like safety, peace of mind, comfort and others. Plan to edit your list as you continue reading this book.

··

A reminder that you can download the free companion workbook to
The Health Advocate's Marketing Handbook from
http://HealthAdvocateResources.com/HABMH

Even though you can't control the perception of your brand, you can take steps to be sure it's at least well-understood specifically by your target audiences, with far less concern about those people who will not care anyway. That's why you need to keep your target audiences in mind when you develop your brand identity. Frankly, McDonalds doesn't target its marketing to vegans because there just aren't enough of them for McDonalds to worry about.

How to Develop Your Brand Identity

Bottom line – as you can see, a brand is more than just its logo. Each brand is a combination of graphics, messages, personality, promises and perception.

Now it's time to begin building your brand identity. We'll begin with some big picture attributes:

- Make sure your brand is clear and understandable. The name Netflix says something about what that company does. The name John's Services does not.

- Be sure your branding is recognizable. Graphically it should be uniquely yours, so don't make it look too much like someone else's. And don't make it so generic that it's not distinctive. That's true for all aspects of the identity, from company name to messages.

- Make sure your branding is consistent. This is the way to establish recognition, not just in the way your logo looks, but in the way you frame your messages, too.

And then – the nitty gritty:

COMPONENT	REPRESENTED BY	NOTES
Your Company Name		Your company name should set the stage for the work you do so people who hear it have some idea of what they will get when they hire you. Obviously, many large companies haven't followed this rule and have been highly successful (e.g. Apple, Google or Amazon). However, unless you have the millions of dollars they had to introduce their brand and have it impact millions of people immediately, you're better off sticking with a name that will be representative of your work. ...more...

COMPONENT	REPRESENTED BY	NOTES
Your Company Name *(continued)*		**Considerations:** Should you use your own name in your company name? See the section on the next page to guide this decision. As you run through possibilities for your company name, be sure to check whether the web address (URL) is available. See Chapter Ten for more information about choosing your URL.
Graphic Representation	Logo Colors Fonts	Unless you are a professional designer, it's best to leave this aspect of your branding to a graphic artist who understands colors, design software and the other skills that will be needed to build your graphic representation. **Considerations:** Different colors represent different emotions. Beyond choosing colors you like, consider what different colors evoke when others see them.[5] Like colors, there are different fonts (types of lettering) that evoke different feelings, too. Choose from serif and non-serif, knowing that some will be easier to read than others. [6] Take a look at your competition's graphic identity to be sure yours is easily distinguished from theirs.
Messages	Positioning Statement, USP, and Keywords	A positioning statement is simply a statement you can use over and over again to represent your business. You might think of it as a tagline. We looked at a few positioning statements in Chapter Three when we talked about promises. Your messages are, of course, far more extensive. You have already developed them in Chapter Three and now you see how they apply to your branding. If you need to, with this better understanding of branding, you may want to edit your messages to be more reflective of the
Attitude or Personality		Your company attitude will likely evolve over time as you grow your business, although it's best to start out with an intention of the direction you'd like it to go.

5   http://www.color-wheel-pro.com/color-meaning.html

6   http://en.wikipedia.org/wiki/Serif

TASK #13

Make notes about the steps you'll need to take to develop your brand identity. Here are some questions to start you off:

1. What words would you want to include in your company name? Make a list of some that would work and would be recognizable. Before you begin, be sure to read the sidebar about using your own name or any other limiting words.
2. Test out possible names with friends, or even better, potential clients.
3. What colors do you like? Check the psychology of colors to be sure you're on the right track.
4. Do you want a tag line (positioning statement) to represent you? It's not vital, but they are nice to have if you can think of one you like and represents your company well.
5. What attitudes represent your form of advocacy? Not just your personality – because that won't necessarily represent your business. You may be a very upbeat, Pollyanna type person, but that may not represent a hospital bill reviewing company well. On the other hand, you might be all business, but find that a friendlier tone is useful for marketing and representing your company.
6. What promises do you want your brand to represent? Refer to the draft promises you began in Chapter Three.

....

A reminder that you can download the free companion workbook to
The Health Advocate's Marketing Handbook from
http://HealthAdvocateResources.com/HABMH

Using Your Own Name in Your Brand

There are a couple of pros, but many more cons to using your own name as part of your company branding.

Pamela's Advocacy Services or Jefferson's Health Navigation Services may make your company sound personal and helpful, but using your own name can actually limit your capabilities over time.

Much of your decision about your name should be based on what your company's goals are, as you defined in your business plan before you even got to this marketing part of your planning. Do you only ever intend to work by yourself and, one day when you are ready to retire, just exit gracefully from your workload?

Or do you hope to grow your business, either in terms of more advocates working under your company's name, locally or in other locations? Perhaps you'll take on partners, or a few independent contractors.

When you build a business, you can also grow an asset – an asset you might sell some day. When you build it as an asset, it's more than just a way for you to earn a living today. It becomes something that has value all unto its own. Part of your nest egg, just like a bank account or a 401K.

If your plan is to grow your company as an asset to sell one day, then using your own name as part of the company name may make it less valuable to your potential buyer. Further, it will make it more difficult for you to transition away from the business when the time comes.

Brands Can Be Ruined, Too

It can take a very long time to build a good strong brand, easily recognizable by your target audiences, and top of mind anytime someone knows they need to call in a patient advocate.

But a brand can be ruined very quickly by thoughtless words, lack of responsibility, bad customer service, or any other misstep. A brand is ruined when you break your brand promise.

Think about Tiger Woods or Paula Deen and you'll know just what I mean. Through bad behavior, their reputations were ruined in a matter of days.

Same with BP, a company highly regarded for decades as providing good service at a fair price. The oil spill off the coast of Louisiana in 2010 has sullied BP's reputation for many years to come.

All companies run into snags from time to time which require them to work on their reputations. But as you build and run your company, you'll want to be sure that your own business practices don't cause a stain on your brand. For small businesses, a bad reputation can spell the end of the road.

If you are torn, and still want to use your own name, then consider branding yourself and your company separately. For example, I have a number of brands – from DiagKNOWsis, which is an umbrella to all my business activities, to AdvoConnection, which is specifically for patients and caregivers, to my own name combined with Every Patient's Advocate – which I have branded for myself, as an individual.

There's no reason you can't do the same thing. So give it some thought. Weigh your options.

• •

Now we've looked at the building blocks of an individual company's marketing strategy:

- Defining and Understanding Target Audiences

- Services, Benefits, and Messages

- Branding

In the next chapter we'll take a look at some overall best marketing practices that are true no matter what your business is. These approaches have been developed and measured over time. The best marketing professionals build them into their work; they are second nature.

Chapter Five
Marketing Best Practices

Anyone can build a website if they learn how to use the software. And anyone can design a brochure without regard to what it should say or how it should be said.

But only the best marketing people understand this list of best practices. When paired with your strategy, and used as the foundation for the tools we'll begin looking at in Chapter Six, you'll be able to develop some highly effective marketing that will help your business become as successful as you want it to be.

Here they are: a baker's dozen of ideas and advice that will give you a good start in developing professional marketing tools that will kick-backside.

1. The three most important marketing decisions you will ever make are: location, location, location.

If you know anything about business, then you know that the same advice is given to almost every aspect of building a business. The point is you need to be in the right location at the right time, whether we are talking about You, the Advocate, being in the right geographical location, or whether your newspaper ad is in the right day's newspaper or your website is connected to the right blogs.

The right location for your marketing is right in front of your target audiences' eyeballs or within their earshot at the appropriate time – the time when they are ready to absorb the message. Success comes from figuring out where those locations are.

The answers can be very simple, or quite elusive. But if you have done a good job of identifying your target audiences, including your influencers, then you will have a much easier time figuring out what locations are right for your marketing.

For example, you may have chosen pregnant women, ages 25 to 40, as one of your target audiences. Now figure out where they are. Are they reading newspapers? Not many are – so running an advertisement in a newspaper is probably not a good tactic for reaching pregnant women. Are they watching TV? Stay-at-home moms might be home with younger children during the day, so that's a possibility. Are they shopping in supermarkets? Yes – but so is everyone else, so that might be a good location, but might be too broad.

If we stretch our imaginations, we can identify some places we'll find pregnant women that might not be obvious at first. You'll find many in daycare centers – dropping off or picking up the children they already gave birth to. You'll find plenty of them reading online support group postings, or hanging out on Facebook. You'll find them oogling over the adorable baby things in baby and toy stores. They, and their baby-daddies and yes, grandparents (influencers!) will be attending baby fairs and expos. Can you think of other places pregnant woman would be that are finite enough that marketing to them, in those locations, makes sense?

That's what you'll need to do for each of your target audiences in order to figure out which locations you'll want to put marketing in. Go wild! Think of all the places they might be and don't eliminate any of them for right now.

One more note about locations. Different locations will require different kinds of marketing. In Chapter Six we will look at the many types of tools you may want to choose from for your marketing. Consider that each location may require a different tool. Plan to create a variety of tools to help you reach them all.

TASK #14

Look at the list of target audiences and influences you made in Chapter Two. For each audience, make a list of places you might find them, whether those are geographical locations, marketing locations or some other easily identifiable place to find them.

....

A reminder that you can download the free companion workbook to
The Health Advocate's Marketing Handbook from
http://HealthAdvocateResources.com/HABMH

---

2. Good marketing is about them, not us.

We looked at this briefly in Chapter Three when we transitioned our list of services into benefits. Benefits are written from your clients' points of view, and that's how most of your marketing needs to be framed, too.

That's all well and good when we are making lists of services and benefits, but we also need to remember this point of view when we write the text for websites, brochures, press releases and other marketing tools.

If you aren't sure about the distinction, then take a look at these two blurbs from brochures for two different advocates. Pretend for a moment that you've just been diagnosed with, say, lymphoma. Which blurb would make you pick up the phone?

BLURB #1:	**BLURB #2:**
ABC Advocates' mission is to help patients who have been diagnosed with a difficult medical problem like cancer or heart disease, to get the help they need. We review test results, provide background knowledge about treatment options, and help patients and caregivers make informed decisions.	Have you been diagnosed with a difficult medical problem like cancer? Or a chronic problem like diabetes or heart disease? Do you need help understanding your treatment options? XYZ Advocates is ready to help you make informed decisions – decisions that will work best for you.

Both of these blurbs represent the same services. Yet, most of us would choose to contact the company represented by Blurb #2 – because we see ourselves in it. If I am reeling from a new cancer diagnosis or am being presented with more than one treatment option and don't have a clue about how to make choices, I want someone to help me who is not only knowledgeable, but benevolent and focused on me, too. Yes – very personal.

3. You must tell your clients what to do and make it easy for them to do it.

Marketers call this a "call to action." Every marketing piece you develop, with the possible exception of your letterhead and business cards, should include a call to action – telling your clients or customers what to do. Here are some examples of calls-to-action:

- Order today!
- Link here.
- Contact us.
- Read testimonials from patients just like you.

Why do we need to tell them what to do? Two reasons. First, to be sure they understand what's expected of them. If you have a brochure that only tells them what you do, and doesn't tell them to call or write, then they may not be so inclined to do so. Remember, many of the people who should contact you are in a state of fear or frustration and aren't thinking so clearly. A concise instruction to do something helps them do it without having to think too much about it.

And second, as a double check on ourselves that we have provided the information they need to be sure they can do whatever it is we want them to do. If I put "Contact Us!" in my brochure, it reminds me to make sure my phone number and email address are available so they'll do so.

Once you've told them what to do, make it easy for them to do it, especially in the case of telling them to contact you.

As someone who has worked as a marketer for 20toomany years, this is the one that drives me the craziest. I go to a website and have to hunt for contact information, only to arrive at a page that has nothing more than a form for me to fill out. Fuggedaboutit.

Now – sometimes that's intentional. For example, I do a lot of writing specifically aimed at empowering patients, but I intentionally make it difficult for them to contact me because I don't work with individual patients. My work is about writing, speaking and advocate business building. If I took calls from individual patients, I would spend all day on the phone with them and would never be able to get my work done. In fact, I make it very clear on some of my sites that I cannot help individual patients by phone.

But at the same time, I make it very clear that I welcome contact from the media to provide advice and expertise. I have an 888 phone number listed, and that phone number lets the caller leave a message, then sends me an email instantly. Since I'm on the road constantly, hooked into email with my smartphone, that's actually much more efficient – I can get back to the caller within minutes.

As a health advocate, you won't want to put any barriers between you and your potential clients. Patients don't pay me anything – so my barriers aren't costing me money. But patients and pregnant women and overweight smokers will pay you! They are looking specifically for your contact information and they will lose patience if you make it too difficult to find.

Be sure your phone number and email address are listed on every page of your website, clearly on your brochure, prominently on any press releases or press kits, and on the last slide of every presentation you might do. That's your bread and butter.

4. The less said the more read.

You have arrived at the "do as I say and not as I do" statement in this book.

But you read that entire sentence right? It made its point – that I am very bad about adhering to "the less said the more read"!

However, this is something that has actually been proven in studies about the amount of information that people will read and remember at one time. Look at these two graphics of newspaper pages:

If you were faced with both pages in a brochure, webpage or flyer, what would you choose to read? To which one did your eyes go first?

This best practice is actually a two-parter. For one, it says that the more whitespace around a piece of information, the more likely someone is to pay attention to it. That means we don't want to crowd website pages or brochures or newspaper ads or billboards with too much text or graphics. Leave plenty of whitespace around it.

And second, edit what you write to make your words clear and concise. I once read a patient advocate's brochure that had one long paragraph comprised of only three sentences, and each sentence said essentially the same thing. Now, emphasis isn't a bad thing, but this was more about filling space (that really didn't need filling) than making sure people could understand what she does.

It should probably go without saying that you'll want to be sure to check your spelling and grammar. In effect, your marketing is your resumé – and you wouldn't hire someone with mistakes in her resumé, right? Don't give your potential client a reason to dismiss you that's unrelated to the work you do. (And please! If you find errors in this book, will you let me know? Despite several editing processes, there are always more typos.)

5. It takes an average 7 to 9 exposures to a brand, product or service before someone will remember it.

For example: A new restaurant called Momma's HomeStyle has just opened in your community. A TV commercial pops up during the evening news, and you may or may not pay attention. Then one day you're driving down the main drag, and there on the corner you see a sign that labels Momma's Homestyle. It sounds vaguely familiar. A few days later you see an ad in the newspaper for the grand opening of Momma's. Later, as you stand on the sidelines at your daughter's soccer game, her teammate's mother asks you if you've tried Momma's yet. Bingo! Now you remember it.

That was only four exposures – and you remember it. Those four exposures came in four different forms: a TV commercial, a sign, a newspaper ad and word-of-mouth.

Of course, my statement said 7 to 9 exposures – average. As you realize, that average must come from other businesses, products or services that require many more exposures to be recognized.

One of the main reasons it takes so long for businesses or brands to be recognized is because they aren't needed right at that time or place by their potential customers.

I could expose you to the name of a motorcycle repair shop a dozen times, but unless you have a motorcycle and it needs repair, you probably won't remember it. Likewise, I could provide the name of a brand of canned collard greens, but unless you enjoy eating collard greens, or find a recipe you're dying to try after seeing it in a magazine (with an ad for collard greens conveniently located next to the recipe) then you'll have no reason to remember it – ever.

Let's take that leap to your advocacy business. Your marketing plan will need to address the fact that a potential client will need to be exposed to your name and your brand at least seven to nine times before it will become memorable. Further, unless that person you've targeted really needs advocacy services at that moment he or she encounters your marketing, he or she may still not remember it. That means you'll need to stay "out there" to be found whenever that potential client is ready to find you.

At least you know that every day, potential new clients will determine they need you. New people will be blindsided by a dire diagnosis, or will learn that their parent has just suffered a stroke, or will be frustrated that their insurance won't pay for a test or treatment, or will determine that a homebirth is just what she wants... That means you need to be constantly positioned for these folks to find you.

An additional way to be sure that seven-to-nine threshold is met more quickly is to develop a variety of marketing tools. Having a number of tools easily available will mean your target audiences will be exposed to your messages in a variety of ways, and they will take note more quickly. If they see a newspaper article about your work, and they can look you up on the web, then download your brochure – that's three exposures, all resulting from the first one.

6. All marketing tools must be consistent and reflect all other marketing.

Your branding, and the way you use your tools, must be consistent across everything you do so it becomes recognizable.

You'll want to focus on consistency in a number of places. Just like your branding, your consistency will be reflected in your graphic look, your messages, and your values. So, for example, if you decide your brochure will have a plaid background, then your website will need that same plaid background. If you use plaid on your brochure but polka-dots on your website and business cards, even if they use the same colors, then they won't be recognizable by your audiences as coming from the same place.

Similarly, if you say "Patient Advocates R Us will accompany you to appointments Monday thru Friday" in your brochure, then you'll want to state it exactly that same way in your website. Meaning, your website can't say "We will accompany you to appointments every day but Saturday and Sunday." Even though the client would draw the same conclusions about the days you can help, your message, framed differently, isn't consistent.

This consistency actually makes our marketing easier. When you write a blurb for a brochure, you can use that same blurb on your website, too. You don't have to reinvent your material each time you develop a new marketing piece.

---

7 http://today.msnbc.msn.com/id/38300339

Should You Include Pricing In Your Marketing Materials?

Since there is no easy answer to this question, I'll give you the pros and cons and some examples to help you make this determination yourself.

Probably the only clear answer is that your marketing materials do need to state that you do charge for your services, and at the very least, potential clients need to contact you for more specific information about the cost. Many patients and caregivers just don't understand that their insurance doesn't cover these services, so be clear up front that you do charge and you'll be happy to disclose more when they contact you. That's a message that will bear repeating in several places.

When it comes to providing pricing information publicly (in your materials) there are dueling concerns for advocates. Studies show that disclosing pricing right up front will result in more calls or emails, and once people do contact you, you have a better opportunity to convince them to hire you. Think about an item for sale in the classifieds, or on CraigsList – you know you're more comfortable about contacting the seller if you already know what the price is.

But advocating and selling used cars aren't even remotely related! And if we look for parallel examples, they are mixed. I often explain the role of an advocate to patients by using real estate brokers as examples. Yes, people can buy and sell homes without the help of a broker, but because they realize those tasks are so fraught with potential potholes, they will ask for a broker's help to protect themselves. By law, brokers must disclose what they will charge for a transaction.

Some advocates see themselves more parallel to a lawyer or a CPA, providing a professional service that is based on the time spent to do the work. In a case like this, you might disclose your hourly rate, and try to give a time estimate. (Although, never—ever– provide an hourly rate in isolation. This is discussed extensively in The Health Advocate's Start and Grow Your Own Practice Handbook. See the Resources in the back of this book.)

Other advocates provide specific services with a set price, such as a health situation analysis that includes a one-hour interview and results in a written assessment, for $x. Or a midwife might provide pre-natal and birthing services for a fixed fee, and might not mind disclosing that up front in a brochure or online. Still others create a sample client with a list of services provided and a total cost. If you decide to do that, be sure you insert prominent disclaimers explaining that it is for illustration purposes only and is not an indication of what it might cost any specific client.

Whether or not you want to provide pricing information publicly is entirely up to you, with the above examples as guidance. If you are still struggling with your decision, and can do so, try including pricing for a month or two, then not including it – see if you can draw any conclusions about this pricing conundrum yourself. Also, Best Practice #10 on page 51 called "Mystery invites inquiry" may help you decide.

7. All marketing tools must refer to other marketing.

In addition to each marketing tool reflecting the others, they should, to the extent possible, refer to each other. For example, you can put your brochure on your website (with the call-to-action – "download our brochure"). Or, your brochure will have your web address (with the call-to-action – "learn more at our website"). I've seen some websites that provide YouTube videos of their latest TV commercials.

As mentioned in #6 of these best practices, by referring one marketing piece to additional marketing pieces, you can shorten that time span for the seven-to-nine exposures needed to make sure people know who you are and how to contact you when they are ready.

8. Timing is everything.

Well – at least it's very important. Timing relates many aspects of marketing. Just like manufacturers and retailers want to be sure their goods are ready way ahead of the holidays, you'll want to be sure you have material prepared for certain times of the year or opportunities.

For example, if you are a weight loss coach, you'll want to pitch a news story, or yourself as an expert, to your local newspaper and TV station right after Thanksgiving. That's when reporters are thinking about the stories they will write the last week in December because they know readers and viewers are gearing up for diet season.

You may not know beforehand when you'll need to step up to take advantage of an opportunity. A senior center may issue a last minute invitation to speak at a gathering, or a national news outlet may call you on a Saturday afternoon and ask if you can talk about the dangers of being hospitalized in July.[7]

As well as you can, be prepared for both marketing opportunities you expect, and those you don't.

9. Manage expectations.

Suppose you see a supermarket ad in the Sunday newspaper and it contains a coupon which will allow you to purchase the large size of an item for the smaller size price. You clip the coupon, and take it to the store.

But others got there before you did – and you find an empty shelf where the large size used to be. So you flag down the young fellow who stocks the shelves and ask him where you can find more of the large size. Sorry, you're told. They're all out. And they don't expect any more to come in. You're out of luck.

How do you feel about that? At the least, you're disappointed. At the most, you're angry. You've lost your regard for the supermarket, and you're going to tell everyone you know about it.

Here's what happened, besides the fact that the market ran out of the large size. **They violated your expectations**. By publishing that coupon, and making a promise, they made you believe you would be getting something you wanted to have. But they didn't deliver.

As an advocate, you'll want to take particular care to frame your messages, including your benefits and services, in a way that can create positive expectations – but only expectations that you can deliver. You never want to make a promise that you can't keep.

You may have heard the admonition – not to "over promise and under deliver." That's great advice. In fact, you may want to turn that around, and plan to under-promise and over-deliver. It will always be better to provide more than you've promised, because people always like to think they've gotten something extra.

However – I would be remiss if I didn't also warn you – that your work must always be the best quality you can deliver. Just like the warning that your brand can be ruined in an instant, so can your reputation as an advocate. Not following through on your promises is the worst violation of expectations possible.

10. Mystery invites inquiry.

The goal of your marketing, believe it or not, is not about making a sale or acquiring a client. Your website or brochure or flyers aren't, by themselves, going to encourage someone to sign a contract with you.

Instead, because someone's health and money are so personal, the best way to convince them you can help them requires a personal approach. As advocates, our best ability to sell our services is to engage in a conversation, maybe by email, but more likely by phone. You have the opportunity to showcase your capabilities, and that gives a potential client the confidence that you are the right person to help.

So that's the real goal of your marketing tools—to provide *just enough* information that they know you *might* be able to solve their FUDGE, but not so much information that they dismiss the possibility; to provide enough answers, but not all the answers.

For example: you might choose to use the word "affordable" when you talk about fees and pricing in a brochure or on a web page. Then, in order to get the real information they want —the cost—they will need to dial the phone, giving you the opportunity to engage. On the other hand, if you include pricing on your website, they might decide it's too expensive before they ever engage with you at all, giving you no opportunity to showcase your abilities.

Yes—it's a little like dating. Remember dating? Not exactly playing hard to get... but maybe just a little bit.

11. Ask for feedback from every client.

One of the very best ways you can improve your service to your clients, and grow your business, is to ask for feedback from every client once your work with them is complete, or after a period of time if you have an extended work relationship. This can be useful in a number of ways:

You can learn what you are doing right. Those "right" things might range from a specific service you offered (reviewing their medications meant they realized there was a conflict) or the way you approach your business (they appreciate that you are upfront about charges, or bluntly honest with their doctor.)

You can also learn what you are doing wrong – which is sometimes even more valuable because it gives you a chance to adjust what you are doing. Mrs. Smith may not have wanted you to reschedule all her doctor appointments for the afternoons (which you did because that's when you could go with her, but made her hungry because she was told not to eat anything before her appointment!) The aspects of your work that turn into negatives for your clients often expose things you didn't know were problematic and aren't even difficult to adjust.

Among the best reasons to ask for feedback is because you can glean testimonials from the responses. Those testimonials can be used in your marketing materials – brochures, your website, during speaking opportunities... they are like gold.

Ask for feedback as you go along by telling clients early in your engagement with them that you'd like to know when things are going well, or when they prefer you take a different approach. Not that you are required to change if they don't like something; in fact, it gives you an opportunity to explain just why you do something the way you do.

Once you've completed your work, you may prefer to give clients a form to fill out that gives them a way to write down their thoughts. You might even put it online if your clientele is more web-savvy.

12. Make sure your message doesn't get lost in the translation.

We all love funny TV commercials. The best ones become the stuff of water-cooler conversations and extended discussion before and after the Superbowl. Having worked in marketing as long as I have, I love to listen to someone's description – "Have you seen that commercial where the guy...."

Once it's been described, we both laugh, and I ask, "And what company or product is that commercial for? What do they want you to buy?"

Try it sometime! For many of the most memorable commercials, that message somehow gets lost! And I'm always amazed, because those companies have huge budgets and well-paid marketing people – but at the end – or an hour later – if you can talk about the commercial but can't answer the question about what it was for (meaning you don't know what company paid for it or what brand was being promoted) then that company really did waste its money.

You don't want to (and can't afford to) waste your marketing money – so don't. Always be sure that your identity is clear within your branding and your message won't get lost in the translation.

13. Each year you will maintain some clients, but you will need to replace others.

Customers or clients come and go. This is true whether your business is a fast food joint on the corner, or health advocacy services. For some businesses, there is more going than coming – a bridal shop doesn't have many repeat customers, nor does a grave stone supplier. And when they do, it's more often for a second bride, or a death in the same family.

Doctors, hospitals, and urgent care centers have plenty of repeat customers / patients. Depending on the specialty or services provided, they may have entire families as customers, Some patients are seen over and over again, like for primary care, or a chronic disease.

As an advocate, you'll need to make an assessment of how likely you are to have repeat customers / patients / clients. If your advocacy services involve accompanying someone to doctor appointments over the course of years, and you do a good job, then that person is likely to be a repeat client over those years. But if your services are geared toward reviewing hospital bills, then you may have some repeat customers (for people who are hospitalized frequently), or you may have many who only ever need you once. If you are a health coach who works on weight loss then, yes, you may have repeat or constant clients. If you make hospice recommendations, then your repeat business will be limited to friends and relatives.

Your marketing plan must accommodate for this reality, too. The way to maintain your good clients is to serve them well for a fair price. That's what good customer service is meant to achieve, and to the extent customer service is considered marketing, you'll want to be sure you handle your work well to keep those patient-clients coming back to you. As long as you can do that, your turnover may be as little as 10% per year, and your marketing will only need to find you that many new clients each year. We'll review some good customer service practices in Chapter Twelve.

But if you need to continually rebuild your clientele, you'll want to be sure to your marketing plan is set up to find new patients on a continuing basis. We'll look at this more in-depth in Chapter Fourteen.

14. Whenever possible, measure, measure, measure.

Marketing is expensive, in both money and time. None of us is rich enough to be able to toss our marketing money at the wall, hoping it will stick, without keeping track of which parts of it do stick.

Measurement of our marketing successes and failures is one of the most important tasks you can undertake to be sure you are investing your marketing time and money wisely.

Some measurement is fairly easy – tracking hits to a website or clipping a story from the newspaper – both are easy to do.

Other measurements are more difficult (or even impossible). As we review each tactic, whenever possible, I'll suggest ways you can measure outcomes from your efforts. They will become even more important once we get to Chapter Fourteen where we'll talk about reviewing and refining your marketing.

■■■■■■■■■■■■■■■■■■■■■■■■■■■■■

So that's it—marketing best practices. In the past five chapters, we have covered a lot of marketing strategy! It's time to apply what we have learned to tools and tactics.

TASK #15

Now that you understand many of the basics about tools and tactics, it's time to clean up some of the work you have done.

Remember that list of places you might find each of your target audiences in Best Practice #1 (earlier in this chapter)? Now go back to them, and put a star next to the most obvious. Just like we identified, then eliminated supermarkets in the example, eliminate those places that are not so obvious, or are more difficult to reach. Later, if you want to come back to them, then do so.

A reminder that you can download the free companion workbook to
The Health Advocate's Marketing Handbook from
http://HealthAdvocateResources.com/HABMH

Chapter Six
The Health Advocate's Marketing Toolbox

Have you ever watched a house being built? Maybe you've seen one in your own neighborhood, or you've watched the DIY Network (that's Do It Yourself) on TV. Building a house takes planning, materials, a piece of land and someone who knows what they are doing.

Just as important, building a house takes tools, each tool with a specific purpose. It would be futile to try to dig a basement or foundation with a hammer. And it would be frustrating and a great waste of effort and money to attempt to install new plumbing with a paint brush.

And so it is with marketing. Effective marketing requires the use of specific tools under specific circumstances. Part of building and executing an effective marketing plan is understanding which tools are available, how to best use them, which ones are worth their cost, and how to be sure they'll have that effect you need them to have – increasing your client base, or expanding the work you do with specific clients.

In the next few chapters, I will describe some of these tools more in-depth. But here we'll begin with a master list to give you an idea of the breadth of tools available. This is not intended to be an exhaustive list of marketing tools or tactics. These are basics that many people ask or wonder about. Marketing can be as expansive or limited as you, or your budget, may choose.

Ratings:

The rating for each tool reflects its importance as part of your toolkit. These ratings are just my own opinion, but they are, for you, at least a start.

    1 is a must have. Do not attempt marketing an advocacy business without this.

    2 is a very-good-to-have-or-do. Your money and efforts will be well spent for the return.

    3 is a develop-or-do-it-if-you-can.

    4 is a forget-about-it-unless-it-falls-in-your-lap-and-you-can-afford-it.

TOOL	RATING	NOTES
Word of Mouth	1	The most effective and important type of marketing there is, word of mouth (WOM) can make or break your business. Knowing that, you'll want to do what you can to shape what those mouths are saying. We'll look at WOM more in-depth in Chapter Seven.
PUBLIC RELATIONS*—See Chapter Eight		
Media Relations	1	Making friends with the people in media who can help you. Making it known you are an expert.
Media Kit	1	Develop a media kit if you hope to be contacted by news people to provide expert commentary.
Press Releases	1	Alert the media with each accomplishment, or for each event.
Pitches	1	Ready for a nice feature story? Hoping the media will expand on an interesting patient story—someone you have helped? You'll want to "pitch" the media.
Newsletters (print or web)	2	See Internet section at right.
Public Speaking	1	This is one of the most effective and fruitful of all marketing tools an advocate can use. Groups of people will buy-in to your expertise.
Trade Shows	2	A great opportunity to expand recognition of your brand with both primary and secondary target audiences.
ADVERTISING*—See Chapter Nine		
TV, Radio	4	
Internet	1	
Newspapers & Magazines	4	The utility of advertising depends on the return for your dollar. This is explained in Chapter Nine with a formula for figuring out what that return might be.
Miscellaneous	1-4	
Promotional Items	3	

* See page 58 for a description of the differences between advertising and public relations

TOOL	RATING	NOTES
INTERNET—See Chapter Ten		
The Alliance of Professional Health Advocates	1	An Alliance membership helps your clients find you, and supports your business tasks so you can concentrate on your advocacy work.
Website	1	Do not attempt to run your business without a website.
Email Signature	1	You'd be surprised what you can promote in an automatic signature at the end of every email you send.
Social Media	2	Blogs, Twitter, Facebook, YouTube – these are all social media. See Chapter Ten for advice about how you can participate, and what you should focus on.
Newsletter	2	Collecting email addresses is inexpensive and reaps big benefits.
PRINT MATERIALS (Collateral)—See Chapter Eleven		
Business Cards	1	Be sure to include your website address and your location if that is important to your business.
Letterhead and Envelopes	2	Invoices, contracts and follow up letters appear more quality-minded and professional when printed on nice letterhead. An inexpensive, acceptable substitute is to use a template on your computer for the same purpose.
Brochures and Flyers	2	Brochures can be considered as print versions of your website (although the approach to develop them will be somewhat different). Use flyers and when you have an event to publicize or even just to alert people that you are available.
MISCELLANEOUS—See Chapter Twelve		
Customer Service	1	How you serve your clients and manage their expectations can make or break your business.
Direct Mail	3	Used here it refers to printed "junk mail" which may, or may not, be appropriate for your target audiences.
Billboards	4	Billboards are not well-targeted and are too expensive for most advocacy businesses.
Personal Notes and Gifts	1	Personal notes are always a good tactic when used as a token of appreciation or recognition.
Volunteering	1-4	Volunteerism is a mixed blessing, depending on where in the formation of your business you are.
Memberships	1	Joining local business or civic organizations is a great way to network and meet both potential clients and influencers.

*The Difference Between Advertising and Public Relations

Non-marketers often get advertising and public relations mixed up. So here's a bit of clarification. (Not that I think you need to be an expert; rather because if you understand the differences, the rest of this book will make more sense).

Both advertising and public relations in this context relate to media – newspapers, TV, radio or the Internet.

Advertising is a way of sharing your message exactly the way you want it shared, appearing exactly the way you want it to look, in a finite space that you have paid for. You might create a TV commercial of exactly 30 seconds in length, then give it to a TV station to air. They will bill you for that 30 seconds of time.

You've seen advertisements in newspapers, too – which fit into certain spaces for which the advertiser has paid by the column inch (one column wide, by one-inch tall.) Those advertisers hoped that when someone read the news on that page, their ad would catch the eye of the reader. The Classifieds section functions the same way except that those ads are surrounded only by other ads, and not news.

Using advertising as a tactic gives you total control of the message and the look. To maintain that total control, you pay for the time or space it takes up.

Public relations is very different in a media context. In public relations you are requesting the media share your information. You provide them with the key points and hope they will distribute it. You might see or hear your information on the news, in a community calendar, or in a newspaper article or a blog. Or you might not.

Through public relations, you have almost no control over the message or the look. Yielding that control means you don't pay anything for the time or space it takes up.

This chapter has presented an overview of what tools are available to us. The next six chapters will describe each of these tools in far more depth.

Chapter Seven
Tools & Tactics: Word of Mouth

Tool: Word of Mouth

Description: The most powerful form of marketing, word-of-mouth (WOM) can make or break your business.

Pros: Potential clients will believe what their friends and family members have to say before they believe what they read or hear anywhere else. Tapping into these influencers can help you grow your business.

Cons: If you have a problem with your business, or if you have trouble with one of your clients, those words will be negative, and potentially harmful.

Devoting an entire chapter to the concept of word of mouth may seem extreme. After all, it's pretty much self-defined, isn't it?

Of course, there's method to my madness. WOM is that important, and there are some tactics that are important to know so you can increase the amount, and guide the conversations that take place about your work and business.

Word of Mouth Can Be Great!

As long as everything that's being said about your company and your work are good, then stand back and let people talk to each other.

Word of Mouth Can Be Devastating!

The problem with WOM, of course, is that you aren't around to hear it all. You can't confirm the right stuff, and you can't deny or correct the stuff that's wrong. And you can't fix someone's negative opinion that has already been passed on.

Here are some ways you can increase the chances of those words being mostly positive and useful for you:

Words Begin from <u>Your</u> Mouth

You may remember the reference in Chapter Three to Elevator Speeches, also known as Elevator Pitches. The idea is that you should be able to sum up your work in 15-30 seconds, the amount of time it might take to get from the top of the building to the bottom of the building (or vice versa!) in an elevator.

Your elevator pitch is based on your positioning statement. The key here is translation and consistency. If you can get used to using the same description anytime anyone asks you what you do, then others will get the hang of that, too. They may not use your elevator pitch verbatim, but they'll use your words. If you use the word "midwife" then they will, too. If you use the word "advocate" then they will, too.

You are influencing their words in a positive way.

Of course, the way those words get shared is through networking – both formally and informally. WOM can take place when a neighbor calls another neighbor and says, "Do you know of someone who can help my mother get to her doctor appointments?" Or it takes place at a large Chamber of Commerce business event among people who have nothing to do with healthcare, but each of which has a story about a parent or a child who has run into a problem with medical care.

Some great networking might take place when you have given a presentation, and someone who attended passes on the fact that she heard you speak, and she thinks her friend's father might benefit from your services.

The best networking, though, takes place when someone who has availed herself of your services tells someone else about what a positive experience it was. Let's look at this possibility a bit further.

Testimonials, Endorsements and Evangelists

In the Best Practices (Chapter Five, #11), I suggested you ask for feedback from every client – both positive and negative.

And the first tactical recommendation I'll make to you in this book is to use, and expand on, the positive client responses by turning them into testimonials or endorsements (which are basically the same thing.) Whether the work you do together comes to an end (hopefully with a healthy patient who no longer needs your services) or if you are in a long-term ongoing relationship – most of the time you will be met with a reply of "of course I will!" when you ask for a reference or testimonial.

You may be able to transform the most gung-ho clients into (what business people call) evangelists. Evangelists are people who are so impressed by your work that they are willing to tell others, on their own, without being asked.

You can groom evangelists to help you. When you find someone who is so enthusiastic, ask him or her if they can suggest a group for you to speak to, and would they be willing to go with you to talk about their experience. Maybe they belong to a church or synagogue group, or they sit with fellow employees around the cafeteria lunch table. If your evangelist is older, you might wrangle an invitation to her senior center.

If you can make that happen, every single person who hears you speak will put you at the top of their list to call when they have a medical challenge or problems with their hospital bills. Even if they don't get sick themselves, they will "evangelize" on your behalf; that is, they will recommend you to their friends. That is word-of-mouth at its absolute best.

Managing Unhappy Clients

Because health is such a personal thing, and because, as a private advocate, you are throwing money into the mix, you will someday have an unhappy client.

Why do I include this in a marketing handbook? Because managing unhappy clients is a form of customer service, and some aspects of customer service can be considered marketing.

I include it here specifically because our topic is word-of-mouth – and there is little that can be more damaging than an unhappy client telling the world about her experience.

The best approach, of course, is to prevent creation of unhappy clients to begin with. Your ability to do that will be based on your ability to manage expectations within your relationship.

Managing expectations is a process that really requires its own book! But some of the basics will help you here. The key is to make sure people know what to expect – good or bad – and to make sure they never have an expectation of a better outcome than is possible.

Here is an example:

> Mrs. Smith has asked to you arrange for her to see Dr. Jones. You make the appointment for Tuesday at 2 PM and tell her you'll go with her. Now, Mrs. Smith thinks she's going to see the doctor, and be home by 3:30 PM to see her favorite soap opera. Unfortunately Dr. Jones is running behind and you never leave his office until almost 4 PM. Now Mrs. Smith is upset with YOU because you are the one who made the appointment and she expected to be home in time for her soap.

> In this case, Mrs. Smith created her own expectation – you had nothing to do with it. But she's angry with you, and tomorrow, she's going to tell everyone she talks to on the phone about all the trouble you caused her.

> So what could you do differently ahead of time? Tell Mrs. Smith that you have made the appointment for 2 PM, but it's always possible the doctor will be running behind. In fact (whether or not you believe this is true), it's possible you'll be there most of the afternoon, because you don't know what tests Dr. Jones might send her for or whether you'll need to pick up a prescription from the pharmacy afterwards.

> In scenario one, you returned Mrs. Smith home at 4 PM, and she was upset. In scenario two, if you return Mrs. Jones home at 4 PM, she'll be happy she got home early. Both scenarios get her home at the same time, but the outcome, and her

regard for you, is very different.

THAT is managing expectations in a very positive way, making both of you more satisfied with the engagement.

Of course, sometimes the happy client ship has sailed – you're way past making that client happy. About the only thing you can do then is try to make it right as best you can. Apologize, maybe don't charge for the time that created the negativity, or you don't charge for the next meeting. Only you will know what's right.

If you can possibly create a less negative scenario, that will serve you well, and when your client speaks about you later – WOM – the edge may disappear. It's about damage control.

If you can't make it better? Then let go of it and go on. Knowing you'll have this unhappy client one day is all the more reason to be collecting those positive testimonials. Balance in all things. But tipping the balance toward the good side is your goal.

Measuring Word of Mouth

You may wonder how something so simple can be measured – how do you know when someone has said something nice about you?

Simply, most of it, you can't – unless someone actually calls you or sends you an email to ask more about your services.

The best way to track word-of-mouth is just to ask. When you are contacted by a possible new client or caregiver, or if someone in the media calls to interview you, or if you receive an email from someone new – ask them how they heard about you. If possible, keep track. Often you'll find the answer is that someone else, perhaps a previous client referred them to you, but sometimes it's no one you've ever heard of that suggested they contact you.

One note about asking where they heard of you... remember the maxim we looked at in Best Practices, Chapter Five that says that people must be exposed to you and your brand between seven and nine times before they will remember you. It's very likely that if you ask them how they heard about you that they will tell you only one place – and usually the most recent one. Just remember that other exposures contributed to the contact being made, too.

You'll see in later chapters that we'll have new ways to measure advertising and other specific outreach you do that will include specific seeding of information, or accessible statistics. But when it comes to measuring word of mouth – just ask.

....

Next up – Public Relations – PR – time to create a buzz!

Chapter Eight
Tools & Tactics: Public Relations

Tool: Public Relations

Description: Outreach to the media to encourage them to promote your business. Tools include press releases, story pitches, event notices, volunteerism and speaking. May show up in print, broadcast or Internet.

Pros: Can be quickly responsive and can provide a level of esteem from being recognized by media. Little money cost; only the cost of time.

Cons: No control over message or timing. You are at the mercy of the media you hope will be interested. They often get it right, but sometimes even "not quite" can be problematic.

Public relations is probably the least understood of marketing activities, yet it can provide the most bang for our marketing buck.

You've probably heard the phrase, "create some buzz." That's precisely what public relations is intended to do. Buzz is simply the topic of conversation. Being the topic of conversation will, in turn, build influence. And influence will have a huge promotional effect on your new business.

Here are some common public relations tools or tactics:

- Press Kits
- Media Relations
- Press Releases
- Event Notices
- Story Pitches

- Newsletters
- Special Events
- Sponsorships
- Speaking

Most PR begins with media, so that's where we'll start.

Hate Bragging?

Contacting the media, and asking them to focus on your work is bragging – yes it is. But it's business bragging and for that, forget what your mother told you about the etiquette of bragging.

Or, better put by one of my first mentors in public relations, "If you don't toot your own horn, no one else will do it for you!"

That's some of the best advice in this entire book.

Press Kits

Prior to our current reliance on the web, press kits were developed to be an expert's marketing to the press – the journalists who could help them tell the world about their expertise. In those days, press kits were usually folders full of individual sheets of different kinds of information -- collateral materials that were all proof of that expertise.

The kinds of materials included in a press kit might have been a resumé, a more narrative biography, copies of previous press clippings, references (other people), some photos (in particular, a headshot), plus brochures or flyers, story ideas and more.

Today experts (like you!) don't really need a printed press kit. Instead you'll want to put these kinds of materials and information on your website.

Your online press kit should contain, at a minimum, your resumé, a high resolution, downloadable photo (ask your graphics or webmaster to help you – the key is that, in order to be usable for print, it needs to be a higher resolution), plus any other material you think will help the media understand what you do and how you can help them. Also, consider including pieces like Frequently Asked Questions and testimonials.

We'll take a more complete look at Press Kits in Chapter Ten.

The Media

We are all listeners or watchers or readers of media. As such, what is our expectation of media?

I believe our expectations are that we will learn something new, or expand on our knowledge about a topic, or find something interesting or entertaining that holds our attention for a period of time. I want my questions answered, I want information that is current and timely, and I want to be able to easily find more information if I am interested further. I suspect your expectations are similar.

When we pair media with public relations, we are mostly focusing on news-type media. When we want the public to know about what we are doing, or what we have accomplished, then we want the media to recognize us in a positive way.

All news-type media conveyed to the general public is comprised of three things:

- News – which mostly takes care of itself. It happens, and it gets covered. Sometimes it can use a little push. See *Events* coming up later in this chapter.
- Advertising – paid space and time.
- Fillers – used to fill the extra space that isn't taken up by the news or advertising.

We – our accomplishments - aren't news – not even when we save someone's life by protecting them in the hospital at their bedside, or when we help a woman give birth in the privacy and peace of her own home.

Advertising isn't news either. It's just parked among news to make people notice it. It's still a good marketing tool, which is covered in Chapter Nine.

It's those fillers that are of most interest to us as advocates. In public relations, we strive to get media to include us in their filler spots, which in turn brings us some esteem – like – hey! We're important enough that they recognized us!

But more than that, it shows all watchers / listeners / readers that we are important enough, and encourages them to contact us – our real goal.

Media Relations and Making Friends

So how do we get ourselves included in those filler spaces? Through some of the tools mentioned previously like press releases, which we'll address in a moment.

However – first we are going to back up to something I think is vital for the most effective public relations campaigns and that is – first, we're going to make friends.

Let's think of it in our own experience. Who are you more likely to do a favor for? A friend? Or a stranger you've never met? More likely you'll do a favor for a friend. And if you need advice, who are you more likely to trust? A friend? Or a stranger?

And so it is with media people – reporters, editors, anchors. Each day they are faced with the challenges of filling in that extra time or space with information people will want to hear or read. They build a rolodex of people they know and trust to provide them with good insight, background information, great quotes and more. Your goal is to get yourself into their rolodex – to be one of their go-to people when the time comes. And further, to be recognized so that when you send them information, they know it's relevant, trustworthy and of interest to their readers, listeners or watchers.

That's what media relations is. Creating that friendship or sense of trust that means you become that go-to person with a strong rolodex position.

How can we develop that relationship? It's really not that difficult. Here are some steps to get there:

1. Identify the media person you want to have a relationship with (one of your target audiences from Chapter Two). It might be the health editor at your daily newspaper, or

the assignment editor at the TV station, or the local talk radio show host. You might begin with the editor of your weekly community newspaper – the one that prints high school sports news and local events - because they are often the easiest to contact. If you aren't sure, then return to our strategic beginnings. Identify the news outlet that is accessed most frequently by your target audiences. (We'll address contacting bloggers and other influential web people in Chapter Ten.)

2. Get that person's email address. If you can't find it published online or in the newspaper, then phone the main desk and ask for it.

3. Send an email to introduce yourself, from his perspective. Here's a suggested format:

> *Dear Mr. Health Editor:*
>
> *Short and to the point – I'd like to become one of your experts when you need a quote, background information or help finding sources. As a local resident, and often easily reachable, I would be able to comment on the following topics:*
>
> * *The Affordable Care Act and insurance issues*
> * *Birthing – the increased rates of Cesarean sections*
> * *Weight loss and its associated hurdles*
>
> *My credentials: I own XYZ Health Advocates. I have 12 years experience in the field and many satisfied clients located throughout the area.*
>
> *I can be contacted at 999-999-9999 or by email at: me@email.com*
>
> *I will follow up in a week or ten days to see if you have questions, but please feel free to contact me in the meantime should the need arise.*
>
> *Best regards,*
>
> *Your Name*
> *Your Signature*

4. Mark your calendar to do that follow up. When you call, be prepared with a topic, perhaps pulled from recent news, or a topic they printed or broadcast recently that you might have been able to address. If the person doesn't answer, then leave a friendly message on voice mail, and call again in two days at a different time.[8] Ask that he call you back (but don't be surprised if he doesn't.) Don't make any more than four follow up calls over the span of two work weeks. Don't be a pest, but always be sure to do what you say you will do.

5. If you do have an opportunity to have a direct conversation, then take advantage of it, but don't overstay your welcome. General chat about topics is good, plus some specific

---

8 Why a different time? All journalists have deadlines and they will likely ignore their ringing phones when they are on deadline. You are hoping to reach them when they aren't on deadline. For that reason, a great way to begin the conversation would be, "I'd like to take just a minute, but want to be cognizant of your time. I hope you aren't on deadline?" That shows that you have focused on them first.

questions such as – how do they prefer to receive press releases and pitches? (email, fax, postal mail) – or – do they have any deadline times you should avoid? And what is their lead time for a story? (These will become clearer later in this chapter.)

At the end, you will either end up with a new media friend/relationship – or you will have struck out. However, don't assume that you struck out if you didn't talk to the person. Over the years I have been very pleasantly surprised to get an email or phone call from someone I thought had brushed me off – and ended up getting some unexpected coverage.

Press Releases

Press releases are simply a heads up to media that you have accomplished something. For health advocacy, you'll want to focus press releases on print and Internet media. The kinds of information press releases are used for isn't typically fodder for broadcast.

Things you have accomplished might be: completion of a training course, opening your business, an announcement that you spoke at a conference, joining a national organization, a new hire or others.

The reasons and formats for press releases have changed just in the past ten years. As more and more people have moved their news-gathering to the Internet, that has been reflected in newspapers and to a lesser extent, TV, radio and magazines.

Reacting to News

Among the biggest holes media people have to fill are putting local spins on national or international news. If you have done your homework and developed your media relations, you put yourself in a great place to be that go-to person when the time comes.

For example – if you deal with patient safety issues, you would have been the perfect person for local media to contact when Dennis Quaid's twins were poisoned with too much Heparin. If you work with patients with traumatic brain injuries, you could have been the expert who commented when Sonny Bono died. If you are an insurance advocate, then you'll make a great quote source for news about healthcare reform.

Even if you haven't groomed your media contacts, if something happens in the news – local, regional, national, even international, and it's something you have credentials and knowledge about, then dial that phone! Call the news editor at the newspaper, or the news assignment editor at the TV or radio station and introduce yourself as someone who is a local expert on topics such as _____ (whatever that piece of news is.)

If they decide to use your expertise, ask them directly to mention the name of your company and be sure to spell your name and company name clearly. For some reason, news people can be really lousy spellers.

Newspapers in particular have changed their former ideas of what is worth printing. With advertising revenue down (see how much thinner newspapers are now?) that means that space for "editorial" (the term used for articles and stories – non-advertising) is down, too.

Knowing that, you can send a press release, but unlike the old days (2008!) that's no guarantee it will get printed. It might! But don't expect it to. Even if it doesn't, it will reinforce your introduction to the media person you've already tried to establish a relationship with.

So how can we improve our chances of getting a press release noticed?

Let's go back to our media person's point of view. Their job is to fill those filler spaces with the information they think their readers/listeners/watchers will want to know about. Their job is not (and I repeat – not) about including something because you sent it.

Knowing that, we want to make our press releases very tailored to their needs. The easier we make their jobs, the better chance they will use our information. So here is how to make it easy:

- Make it sound just like what you read or hear from them. There is a certain cadence to any given newspaper's articles. The first sentence will answer who, what, when and where. The rest will answer why.

- Make it relatively short and concise. Space and time are at premiums, so if you edit yourself, they won't have to.

- Attach a photo. Maybe they'll use it, maybe not. Look at other photos any print media uses to see what kinds of photos they like and submit one that looks similar (except with you in it, of course!) Be sure the photo is at least 200 dpi. The higher the resolution the better. (If you aren't sure what that means, check with your graphics or web person.)

- Make your contact information very prominent so they can contact you for confirmation or extra questions. Include phone and email.

- Be sure to link to your website. Always include a link to your website "for more information." You'll understand the importance of this in Chapter Ten.

Find a press release formatting example in the free handbook that accompanies this book, located at http://HealthAdvocateResources.com/HABMH.

How should you send a press release? These days (again – a change from the old way of doing things) most reporters prefer email. However – if you have taken the "making friends" steps from earlier in this chapter, then you will have exactly the information you need about how to send them the information.

Story Pitches

A story pitch will be regarded somewhere between the news and filler. It's a bigger story than something you have accomplished. It involves more people, and at least one of those extra people must be someone others can relate to. It will bring far more attention to you and your work than a press release will.

PR pros will tell you a story pitch needs a "hook" – defined as the attention grabbing idea behind your story idea. The hook is what compels someone to be interested and may consist of a shocking statement, a human interest concept – anything that garners the response of "Wow! I didn't know that!"

For advocates, story pitches will be mostly human interest stories that blend a real problem readers and listeners have with a solution – you. If your story is about someone with melanoma, then anyone who has melanoma, has lost someone to melanoma, or fears getting melanoma will be paying attention.

Your approach will vary a bit from a press release. Here's an approach to pitching a story:

1. Write out your story for yourself, including the hook you think will be attention-grabbing. Choose a client you've had success with, and write the problem, the solution, and your role in providing the solution. The more dramatic, the better. The more universal the medical problem, the better, too – because more of that media person's audience will be able to relate. A patient story that begins before (working with you) with a positive outcome after (working with you) is a good slant.

2. Make sure the person whose story you are telling is willing to share that story publicly. Media won't tell your story without having that person to focus on. If you have two people with similar stories, then plan to provide media with access to both and let them choose which one is more compelling. Don't make any promises about stories to your clients. In fact, manage their expectations by telling them specifically that you make no promises. Otherwise, the news outlet may decide to leave your person out, and that person might get upset with you!

3. Next, put your story into an easy and brief format for the media person you will pitch it to (hopefully someone with whom you have established a relationship, described earlier in this chapter.) Here's a suggested format:

   a. Synopsis: A 2-3 sentence synopsis that describes your story – the situation the client was in, the challenge, what you did to help, the client's status today. Make it sound dramatic! And be sure your hook is front and center.

   b. More Information: an expanded version of the story

   c. Your client's contact Information, including the statement that your client is willing to be interviewed, with complete name, phone and email address.

   d. Your complete contact information.

   e. If there is something else that make the story timely, include it here. For example, if Patient Safety Week is coming up, you might mention that to accompany a story about a patient you helped who had acquired a hospital infection.

TASK #16:

Think of clients you have had with good stories that put you in a good light. As I said, the more dramatic, the better. Make a list of stories you can expand on for a story pitch.

....

A reminder that you can download the free companion workbook to
The Health Advocate's Marketing Handbook from
http://HealthAdvocateResources.com/HABMH

Timing

Don't forget one of our best practices from Chapter Five. Timing, for PR opportunities, is very important, in two different ways.

First, you'll need to be wary of deadlines. You'll want to be sure to give them plenty of lead time. If you are pitching a story to a newspaper, give them a month. If pitching to a monthly magazine, pitch four to five months (yes – months) in advance.

You also want to be sure not to try to contact them when their deadline is tight, because they'll be too busy to talk to you. When you are doing your outreach to establish relationships with media people, timing is a good thing to ask about. When a media person realizes you are smart enough to ask about her deadlines, and therefore what times to adhere to – or avoid – then she will know you really do get it – and she'll be more likely to put a big star next to your name in her rolodex.

Put all this information together to send to your media contact.

If you send it as an email, include it in the body of the email. Don't write it in a separate application to attach to the email because many media email systems will strip attachments or deliver your email to spam. In the subject line, include something like: "Story Idea: In time for Patient Safety Week" or "Story idea about choosing a new insurance plan" - something to give the reporter a reason to open the email. If you can write a succinct version of your hook as the subject, that's even better.

Mention in the email that you will follow up in a few days if you don't hear back. Then do so, following the advice in the Media Relations section of this chapter.

Event Notices

There are two kinds of event notices – before the event and after.

After is easy – it's an accomplishment, so it gets handled just like the press releases described earlier in this chapter.

However, if you want to invite the general public to an event, or if it's a big event and you want the press to cover it (for them to cover it, it needs to be huge, involving at least hundreds, if not thousands of people, or they will ignore it) – then send an event notice.

Most media outlets still include community calendars in their publications or during local programming. Find out who the calendar person is, get that email address, and include the event details in your email. Check them out ahead of time to find out what their format is, and don't bother including additional details because they won't print or broadcast them.

Note: This information holds true for programs that are free and open to the public. If you will be charging admission, then they probably will not include it on their community calendars.

Newsletters

Newsletters can play an important role in your public relations efforts. There are two ways to send a newsletter – by postal mail, or by email. Your choice depends on your target audiences. Due to cost and effort, you will probably want to create an electronic (email) newsletter. However, if your audience is older, say 75+, and they are truly the people who would hire you (as opposed to their adult children hiring you) then preparing and distributing a printed, postal mailed newsletter might be a great marketing tool for you.

We won't spend time here discussing the differences between electronic and postal newsletters, because there just won't be that many advocates who will make use of printed, postal mailed newsletters. If you do want to create one, then you can follow some of the content rules for emailed newsletters, even though the method of sending them will be different.

You'll need four things for an effective newsletter, whether it's printed or electronic:

1. mailing addresses

2. an application for sending them (Check the resources at the end of this chapter.)

3. a good newsletter design

4. great, compelling content to interest the receivers, and to help them remember to call you when they need an advocate

Collect email addresses whenever you can. Add a place to your website for people to sign up. When you speak, let people sign up to receive your newsletter. If someone contacts you for advice, add them to your email list. Whenever you can add an email address, as long as you know the receiver won't object, you improve your chances of being hired.

Casting a Wider Net

If your target audiences are located beyond your local region, you'll want to become familiar with some of the ways you can be found as a resource by journalists far and wide.

HARO and PitchRate:

These organizations give you the opportunity to reach out to journalists, radio hosts and others just by signing up with their services to receive email notifications. Journalists make requests for specific kinds of experts, and when you can help them, you respond. Two such services are free: HARO—Help a Reporter Out (www.helpareporter.com) and PitchRate (www.pitchrate.com). Be sure to abide by their rules for responding, though. If you respond to something that's not really your expertise, you'll get bounced from their email list.

Press Releases:

When you prepare a press release, if you think it has a bigger picture reason to be publicized – more than just your local area (for example - if you've won a national award), then you may want your release to go broader. In addition to paying press release services (which are used by the likes of the Associated Press or the Wall Street Journal) such as PRWeb.com and PRNewswire.com, there are some free press release distributors. PRFree.com and Free-press -release.com are two of them.

If you go the free distribution route, don't really expect any media to pick them up and republish them. If they do – bonus! But what you can expect is that they will appear online, and will link back to your website – a very good thing, as you'll see in Chapter Ten.

A word about opting-in. Email etiquette, and most email applications, require users opt-in; that is, they must specify that they want to hear from you - they choose the "opt"ion of getting email from you. When you actually send an email through the service, whether it's a newsletter or not, they will also be given the opportunity to opt-out. This also means you'll need to use your discretion about adding email addresses when someone hasn't opted-in. Personally, when someone writes to me for advice, I think it's fair to add them to my list. But if you add email addresses arbitrarily, you can be reported for spamming – and that decreases your chances of getting your email received by the people who really do want to hear from you.

The second requirement, an application for sending out your newsletters, is a cost. Services like Constant Contact or iContact will charge you for the ability to send email through them. It seems expensive, but it's truly worth the cost because they make sure your emails get delivered and not spammed. Further, you can track and measure who is reading which parts of your newsletter. They tell you which links were clicked on, whether someone forwarded the email – all kinds of behind-the-scenes information. These programs aren't infallible – sometimes there are hiccups, believe me! But for now, their systems are the most effective and efficient for sending an email.

Design – you can guess – needs to be branded and consistent with all your other marketing. If you can't develop it yourself, then ask your graphics person to set you up with a template you can use over and over again.

Content – the real meat of your newsletter. If you don't have articles and information that people care about, then it won't matter how well the other components work because people will either opt-out or just hit the delete button when your email arrives.

To maximize the readability of your newsletter, you'll want to create excellent, actionable and/or interesting content. Be consistent with your content; for example, you may want to include a success story in each newsletter, accompanied by a description of a service you offer, maybe an editorial about something that has happened in the news (and what your services would have meant to improve the situation) – compelling content.

There are two approaches to including the content in your email newsletter. If you have a number of pieces to it, then include just a few sentences about each, then link to the rest of the story on your website. If you have only one or two pieces of content, then go ahead and include the entire piece in your newsletter.

Just like any piece of marketing, and as we reviewed in Chapter Five about Best Practices, don't forget to include easy to locate contact information. After all, the whole reason you're sending a newsletter is to encourage people to hire you.

✦Public Speaking

I truly enjoy public speaking – and maybe you do, too. It's not everyone's cup of tea, but if you are OK with standing in front of a crowd, and you can hold their attention for a period of time, then speaking is an excellent – really excellent – public relations tool.

Finding opportunities (gigs) doesn't need to be difficult. Start with a group you know, depending on your target audiences. If you work with older people, you can contact a local senior center. If your clients are pregnant women, find them in daycare centers. You've made a list in Chapter Two – this is a time to use it. If you want to, you can even set up your own presentation in a church or school auditorium. Publicize it well and people will come. Once you get started, different groups will begin to call you because they network with each other.

The topics you offer will also depend on your audience. Sometimes the program chair of a group will call you and ask you to speak on a specific topic.

Here are some hints for giving good presentations:

- Be well prepared ahead of time. Know your subject matter.

- **Powerpoint or no Powerpoint?** That is the question. Microsoft Powerpoint is a great tool for creating slides to illustrate your talk. If you can improve the quality of your talk, then use it – but not with a lot of text; rather, graphics that illustrate what you have to say. Do NOT stand in front of a group and read from Powerpoint slides! There is no quicker way to turn off your audience.

Not a Big Fan of Public Speaking?

The rewards for speaking to groups can make a huge difference in the success of your marketing outreach. Speaking to groups of your target audience gives them a very personal glimpse into who you are as a person, creates a level of trust, and makes it very easy for them to pick up the phone to hire you.

If you are nervous, but want to give it a try, then start with small groups. Maybe you can round up a small group at your church or synagogue, or see if a local daycare center would be willing to let you speak one evening to a group of parents. The leader of a support group for cancer patients might invite you, or you might address a group on a Sunday afternoon in a nursing home (when adult children come to visit.)

Start small if you must, but give strong consideration to speaking as a marketing tactic.

- Be flexible – you never know when the time they have given you to speak will grow longer or shorter.

- Let people ask questions either during or after. I prefer during because that's when someone thinks of the question. But I also ask them to be mindful that we need to move on or we won't finish – and I must often cut people off because they all want to tell their stories.

- Have handouts prepared that contain your contact information and some bullet points from your presentation.

There are entire books written about effective speaking – or just do a search online for "effective presentations" to see what they say. The *Advanced Marketing Handbook* (available mid-2014) will have an expanded chapter about Public Speaking.

There are few marketing tactics that are so public and personal all at the same time as speaking is. That's why it's so effective. Jump in!

Other PR Tools and Tactics

This is by no means a comprehensive list of PR tools and tactics. I've included just the ones you will likely want to use as a health advocate.

You may have other ideas that fall under the category of PR. If so – great! And I would love to hear about them. (Find my contact information in Chapter Sixteen - Resources.) Or, you may simply find that they've been included in another category in this book.

Truth is – it doesn't matter what we call it, as long as it works.

Measurement - Tracking Your PR Efforts

One of the most fun aspects of public relations is tracking your outcomes. You'll want to know whether your efforts have paid off. Knowing whether or not your information has appeared anywhere is the first measurement, and most of the time, it's not too difficult to find out.

Obviously, the best way to track your press release and story outcomes is to watch your TV, listen to your radio, or pick up your newspaper and clip your story from a print publication when it appears.

Even easier are the mentions that show up online. These days, most newspapers, TV and sometimes radio are fairly easy to track online, and of course, web mentions are even easier.

You don't need to check each outlet you've approached individually. Simply set up Google or Yahoo News Alerts, and your results will be delivered to your email.

Setting up these News Alerts isn't difficult. Go online to either Google or Yahoo and look for their news sections. Follow the instructions for getting alerts sent to your email address, using your specific keywords – those you developed in Chapter Three.

If you have trouble setting them up, I've written out a step-by-step procedure for doing so, along with some best practices. Find that procedure online at: http://bit.ly/newsalertsetup

You can also check the number of hits and pageviews on your website.* See Chapter Ten to see how this tracking takes place.

The best measurement, of course, is finding emails or phone messages from potential clients. Just like we discussed in the Word of Mouth Chapter (Seven), make it a habit to ask everyone who contacts you how they heard about you and your services.

Chapter Nine
Tools & Tactics: Advertising

Tool: Advertising

Description: Inclusion of your messages in any form of media, usually paid. TV commercials are advertising – a business buys a specific amount of time and provides the exact message (video and audio) to be aired. Another company buys space in a newspaper, providing their logo, plus the exact words and contact information they want the newspaper to put in that space.

Pros: Exact control over what the viewer / reader / listener sees and hears. Relatively easy to measure success or failure of ad to attract business.

Cons: Most advertising is pay-for-placement. It can be more or less expensive. The advertiser must pay for the time and space the ad uses, plus the content itself (graphic, audio and/or video).

As we learned in Chapter Six, what distinguishes advertising from other forms of marketing is that we get mostly total control over the message, but we pay for that control. That payment comes in the form of dollars far more than time. Those dollars go toward two things:

1. Creation of your ad
   An ad must be created, using your brand, including the right message targeted to one of your audiences, placed in the right medium, then measured for success.

2. Payment for the space (measured in inches, pixels or time)
   Depending on the medium, you'll either print or broadcast your ad – newspapers, magazines, radio, TV or online. Each of those media charges for the space, by the column inch (one column wide by one inch tall), by the square inches, or by 15 second increments (30 seconds, 1 minute).

Components – What Goes In that Ad?

Maybe you used to watch Jay Leno's Headlines. They were a mixture of newspaper headlines and advertising that people have clipped and sent to him. When he showed an ad, I laughed out loud! And then I realize somebody paid good money for that ad. Except that they got a little extra mileage out of showing up on The Tonight Show, they had really wasted their money.

What does belong in an ad? No matter whether you're making a TV commercial or a small display ad, there are some specific components that should be included to be sure you're getting the most from your advertising dollars.

- **Your brand** – represented by your logo and tagline. If it's a color ad, then be sure the colors are correct.

- **One message** – and one message only, which includes your call to action. It can be one sentence or a little more, but keep it brief and succinct.

   Call today to learn more about our approach to keeping your loved one safe in the hospital.

   Doulas help keep Mom and baby safe and comfortable. Learn more at our website.

- **Contact information** must be included – phone number (include your area code just in case someone needs it, especially online), email address and website.

- **A promotion** can help you light some fires and can be part of your call-to-action. You might promote a free 20 minute assessment, for example. There aren't a lot of discounts or giveaways a patient advocate can provide. But people do like to feel they are getting some kind of deal.

- **A measurement vehicle** – this is how you'll know whether your money was well spent. It's so important, we're giving measurement its own section – coming up.

- Don't forget **white space** – in Chapter Five we talked about white space – making sure the elements of your printed materials have space so they'll be noticed.

Measuring Your Success

One big advantage to advertising is that it is very measurable. If you run an ad and your phone begins ringing off the hook, it's probably not a coincidence. On the other hand, if you run an ad and nothing changes, then that tells you something, too.

Beyond just timing – your ad runs, your phone rings – there are other ways to measure your success, too. You've probably seen measuring mechanisms but didn't know that's what they were. For example, a TV commercial might say "Ask for Manny!" Now, there may not be anyone who works there named Manny. But it signals them that you are calling because you saw that TV commercial. They might be running a newspaper ad at the same time, that says "Ask for Chester!" If you call and ask for Chester, then they know you saw the newspaper ad – not the TV commercial. Depending on how many calls they get for each, they can assess which worked better – the ad or the commercial.

Similar to the "Ask for!" technique are direct mail campaigns (you know – the junk mail that arrives in your mailbox) that tell you to send your check to "Dept 467" (believe me, there is no Department 467). Now that you know what they are, you'll see them everywhere.

You might even use this kind of tactic yourself. You might not want to tell people to ask for Manny, but you can add "Ext. 6" to your phone number to any ad campaign – even if you don't have an extension 6.

If you advertise only in one place, and the phone begins ringing, then you know why. But if you have multiple places you advertise, then you do want to track them so you can figure out if your money is well spent.

Frequency

You may remember in Chapter Five Best Practices, I told you that someone must be exposed to your marketing between seven and nine times before they will remember it.

In addition to that challenge is one aspect of advertising that is very important, and that is, repetition. Your branding must be repeated – we've covered that – but your specific ad must be repeated many times, and in a variety of locations, too.

Repeating your ad many times is a must when you choose advertising as a marketing tactic. That may mean running your ad many times in the newspaper, every day for a month. Or it may mean airing your TV commercial during a few different shows your target audiences probably watch each day. It's that repetition that will make it memorable.

A further fly in the frequency ointment is the ability for people to look past your ads. They glance at the newspaper, and unless an article catches their eye, then your ad probably won't. Or they get up from the TV during a commercial in order to get something to eat – or worse, blow past your ad because they've recorded the show your ad is scheduled to run on, and when they watch it later, they fast forward to skip the commercials. Or they're driving along, listening to the radio, and push the button to change stations once the commercials come on.

All this means that, as part of your advertising planning, you must be sure to repeat your ads many times. You'll find that the representatives for the media you want to advertise in will have suggestions for how to do this, the right timing for doing it, and packages that improve the pricing per ad exposure.

Listen to your media reps, and compare their packages to each other. They will, of course, suggest you do much more (and spend much more money) than you have to. But they do want you to succeed with your advertising because if you find it has worked for you, then you'll return another time to do more advertising.

Figuring Cost vs Return

No matter which form of advertising you decide to do, you'll need to decide whether the cost is worth the return. If you spend $100, what is the likelihood you'll get your $100 back, plus the extra your advertising was intended to bring in?

Figuring this out will be little more than an educated guess.

However, here's an approach to make sure it's more educated and less guess. As you estimate these amounts, err on the very conservative side. You'd rather be pleasantly surprised that you spent less and made more money, than to learn that your estimates were way off in the wrong direction.

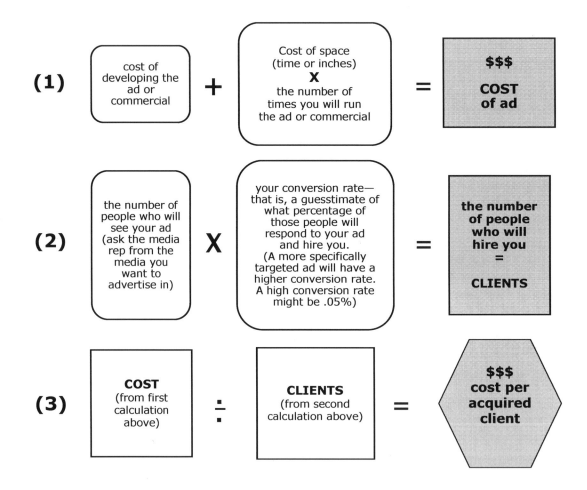

(1) cost of developing the ad or commercial **+** Cost of space (time or inches) **X** the number of times you will run the ad or commercial **=** **$$$ COST of ad**

(2) the number of people who will see your ad (ask the media rep from the media you want to advertise in) **X** your conversion rate— that is, a guesstimate of what percentage of those people will respond to your ad and hire you. (A more specifically targeted ad will have a higher conversion rate. A high conversion rate might be .05%) **=** **the number of people who will hire you = CLIENTS**

(3) **COST** (from first calculation above) **÷** **CLIENTS** (from second calculation above) **=** **$$$ cost per acquired client**

Once you know your cost per acquired client, you can decide whether you will be able to make a profit from running that ad. Will you make enough money from that client to cover your time, all your work expenses, AND the cost of acquiring that client? This will help you decide whether advertising is where to put your marketing money.

Making these guesstimates won't be easy. You'll have to get some information from the medium you want to advertise in. For example, TV, radio and daily newspapers all have audited numbers to share – from Neilsen, Arbitron and other companies that figure out how many people are reading, watching or listening. For weekly papers or websites, you may have to take their word for the numbers of readers, although they may be able to provide you with some documentation.

Most non-marketers are surprised to know how small the "conversion" percentage is. Conversions are the number of people who experience your ad vs. the number of people who take action. You must remember, too, that the number of people who take action won't even be the number of people who hire you. But they will be driven to call you or check out your website, giving you the opportunity to sell them on your service.

And don't forget, as we learned in Chapter Five, someone needs to be exposed to your advertising or PR or signage or anything else between seven to nine times to even remember your name.

While figuring all this out is a task you can undertake yourself, you might have more success getting someone who really knows advertising to help you. But be careful who you ask. The person who sells advertising for your weekly newspaper might know something about how you should advertise in her newspaper, but she knows a lot more about how her commission will be paid from your ad. Better to find someone, like a one-person or small business marketing person, who will be much more objective.

Where Should You Advertise?

Let's look at the various kinds of advertising to help us decide the "where". These descriptions are focused on smaller advocacy businesses, so if your business is larger (more than 10 advocates in your group) then you might consider expanding the recommendations.

TV and radio commercials: These are very expensive and out of reach for most health advocates. Even a decent quality commercial can be very expensive to put together (TV more so than radio.) the cost for space might sound good – as little as $50 or $100 for a one minute commercial. But that one minute is fleeting, you won't be sure when they are going to run it, and when that minute has passed – then it's gone. If you do the math and decide these commercials will work for you, then plan to run the same ad as many as 25 or 30 times to make sure you get your money's worth.

One additional note. As DVRs and TIVOs are more frequently attached to TVs, fewer TV commercials are actually being seen, no matter whether they are on cable, a satellite dish or broadcast. It could be your wonderful TV ad will be skipped entirely.

Newspapers and magazines: Depending on the newspaper, these ads might be a good choice for you, a health advocate. Of course, the more one of these print media is targeted to your specific audience, the better. A small, community or suburban newspaper might be a good choice if you know there are plenty of adult children of older people, or families who could use your assistance. In my area, we have a monthly magazine targeted to families with children, and another one targeted to Seniors. Running a box ad (called a display ad) in one or both of these could work well, depending on the advocacy work you do and the cost of the ad.

If your organization is larger, and your daily newspaper has one day focused on your particular audience (my daily newspaper runs a health section on Tuesdays) then an ad on that particular day might be worth the expense.

A word about classified advertising – unless you are trying to sell your car, boat, motorcycle, home or even your jet, forget newspaper and magazine classifieds. No one is looking for services there anymore; they are looking for things they want to buy. On second thought, forget about your jet, too.

Online advertising: The biggest problem with online advertising is knowing how many people will see your ad before it's run so you can be sure you're getting the eyeballs you're paying for. (Yes, seriously, that's how online marketers phrase it - determining how many eyeballs will see it.) As stated earlier, for smaller, very targeted websites, it's sometimes difficult to get solid numbers ahead of time (although larger websites usually do have these numbers for you.)

One place you can do some online advertising and control your budget is through Google's keyword advertising. You choose specific keywords, "patient advocate" and "Boston", for example. When someone searches for those keywords, your ad comes up at the top of the page. (Don't forget – you began developing your keywords in Chapter Three.) If someone clicks on your ad, then you pay Google for that click. You will know how much the cost per click (CPC) is in advance, and based on that, you can set a budget with Google. Once there have been enough clicks to meet your budget, your ad will no longer appear until you go back to Google and set up a new campaign. You can learn more about Google's AdWords program[9] to see if it's something you think makes sense for your business.

If you decide to place print or broadcast ads or commercials, you may find they also package those ads with online ads which are placed on their websites. It could turn out that the online placement is more fruitful for you than the actual newspaper or TV ad. It will certainly be more measurable, so be sure to ask your media rep about their approach to measurement feedback – how will they let you know how many people are viewing your ad online?

There are other great ways to advertise your services online. Beyond running ads on other sites, you can (should!) have your own website, be writing a blog, participating in social networking, even podcasting and more. These aspects of your promotional tactics are so important they have their own chapter (Chapter Ten.)

Some Miscellaneous Advertising Possibilities

Promotional Items - giveaways like pens and pencils or notepads or stress balls with your company logo. These might be useful if you are giving a talk and want to leave people with

---

9   http://www.google.com/adwords/

a useful reminder about how to get in touch with you (when they are ready), or if you intend to set up a booth at a health, senior or baby fair or trade show.

Billboards – are very expensive and not a good option unless your company is quite large. There is the cost of design, plus the cost of creating the billboard itself, and then you'll pay by the month or year.

The Yellow Pages – printed version - are tres passé for most businesses, but if your primary target audience – the people who will write checks for your services – are seniors, then you might consider a Yellow Pages ad. (If your audience is any younger, then forget it. Too expensive for too few eyeballs.)

Low and No Cost Advertising for Health Advocates

Besides the price tag, the best thing about low and no cost advertising is that the return on your investment can be huge. If you spend $1 and you get $100 worth of business, then you are getting a 1,000% return on your money!

Here are some possibilities that can have a huge return. As long as you don't have huge expectations, they might be worthwhile.

1. Those newspaper classifieds I suggest you skip are now found on Craig's List. **Craigslist.org** let's you put an ad online that costs you nothing except some time to set it up. This would work if you do legal work for patients, or even insurance work, since there are sections for each (under Services.) There doesn't seem to be a category for medical or birthing services – yet. Who knows – by the time you read this, maybe there will be.

   However – a warning – if you decide Craigslist might work for you, learn about the possible hazards, including scam artists and murderes who might contact you. Do a search engine search for 'Craigslist, cautions" – and read the suggestions for staying safe with Craigslist ad responses.

2. A few other low and no-cost options might work well for you. Church bulletins, community newspapers and billboards, employee newsletters, senior center bulletins – many of these run very low cost ads, but they might reach your target audiences very well.

3. **Email signature** – after your closing on your email, add the information you include on your business card. You can set these up to happen automatically in most email applications.

4. **Your "on hold" or voice mail message** on your phone – why not include a small enticement, or at least a very polite "we're glad you called and look forward to helping you with _____." If someone must listen to your message, it might as well be pleasant and promotional.

5. **Signage** – you don't need a building or store-front to use signage. You've probably seen cars and small trucks with logos painted on them. That may be more than you want to do, but for no more than $50 or so, you can get a sign shop to put your logo, tagline and phone number on a magnetic sign that will adhere to your car doors. Put them on or take them off at will.

And of course, **printed material** that you can hang up or leave behind – on bulletin boards, telephone poles, and other places where your target audiences are likely to find them. Many of them can be printed right from your own computer at little or no cost to you. For more about these printed materials (collateral) see Chapter Eleven.

Cross-Promotional Advertising:

Let your imagination run with this very low cost way to promote your services. You and another business will promote each other.

Find another business that can be complementary to yours. Each of you makes up a small flyer to distribute to all your prospective clients or customers. For example, in the "old" days, you used to find a flyer for the local video rental store stuck to the top of your pizza box. If you went to the video rental store, you'd find a flyer for the pizza store stuck in the bag you took home with your rented video in it.

Advocates can pair up with associated organizations, or even some that aren't really associated, but might service similar clientele. My hair dresser volunteers for an organization that provides wigs to breast cancer patients who lose their hair through chemotherapy. She could give out flyers about my advocacy services, while I let all my potential clients know about her hair salon services.

Now it's up to you to decide where you want to spend your advertising budget. You may find many more possibilities than we've looked at here. Let your imagination be your guide – with your target audiences in mind.

TASK #17:

Review the explanations in this chapter along with the table in Chapter Six to make a list of the advertising possibilities you would like to explore. No definite decisions yet. This list will be those advertising tactics worth looking at more closely.

....

A reminder that you can download the free companion workbook to
The Health Advocate's Marketing Handbook from
http://HealthAdvocateResources.com/HABMH

Chapter Ten
Tools & Tactics: On the Web

Tool: Internet / Web

Description: From websites, to social media (blogs, Facebook, Twitter, YouTube and others) to email and online direct mail – the Internet is an advocate's best option for promotion, second only to Word of Mouth.

Pros: Relatively inexpensive, unlimited scope, fairly easy to find and promote to your target audiences, and for target audiences to find you.

Cons: If your target audience isn't online, then you'll miss them entirely. This is also where you'll find the most competition – both your direct competition and competing interests – so many things going on online to compete for attention.

Get comfortable. Make a cup of tea. Find a pencil to take notes. And hang on – this is going to be a very long chapter.

The growth of the Internet since the mid-1990s has changed the face of healthcare in ways we never could have imagined even ten years ago. Adoption of the Internet by the many people who can use to it to do everything from ruin their lives (pornography and gambling) to saving their lives (maybe by contacting you) continues to grow daily.

You'll remember the mention of location, location, location in Chapter Five. Well – the Internet is prime real estate. It's a health advocate's Board Walk or Park Place. It must be respected and nurtured as THE place that will deliver the majority of your business to you, second only to word-of-mouth. Beyond your capability for using it to research the many aspects of care that can help your clients, it will be your prime resource for attracting new clients.

We're going to take a look at most important online tools you can use to build your advocacy business, the pros and cons, estimated costs, and what you need to keep an eye on for the future.

(A reminder that this discussion is only about marketing. An entire book could be written about the many ways you can manage your business using the Internet, too.)

Here are the Internet tools we'll review:

- The AdvoConnection Directory (through the Alliance of Professional Health Advocates)
- Your website
- Search engine optimization (SEO)
- Blogs

Let's get started!

The AdvoConnection Directory and The Alliance of Professional Health Advocates

(Yes – this is the biggest shameless plug in this book. But now that you know something about marketing, you can appreciate why it's here.)

AdvoConnection is an online directory of private, independent health advocates located throughout the United States and Canada. http://www.AdvoConnection.com The people found in the directory are all members of the Alliance of Professional Health Advocates.

No matter what else you as a health advocate do to market yourself, you must be listed in the AdvoConnection Directory, because, with 3,000+ new patient and caregiver visitors each month, it enjoys more traffic than any individual advocacy website. Patients or caregivers search for free, requiring only an email address and zip code. Then the patient or caregiver checks off the kinds of assistance they are looking for and – viola! – they find an advocate to help. They'll find you if you are listed as an advocate who provides those services in their location.

You cannot be listed in the AdvoConnection Directory unless you are a member of the Alliance. APHA (also called The Alliance) is a membership organization specifically designed to help health advocates grow their businesses. It offers multiple types of business support, including the abilities to network with other advocates, get liability insurance, have legal or medical questions answered and, most germane to this book, get marketing advice.

You may belong to, and participate with the Alliance no matter how much training you have, whether or not you are certified or credentialed. It's intended to be your support to grow your business.

> The Alliance is found at http://APHAdvocates.org
> AdvoConnection for patients is found at: http://AdvoConnection.com

Why am I so high on AdvoConnection? Because I'm the founder – the person who launched the site in 2009—and because I am passionate about making sure patients get the help they need. When I went through my odyssey with the healthcare system, there was no one I knew of who could help me outside the existing MD / hospital setting. As the American healthcare system continues to become more difficult to navigate successfully, patients will need advocates more than ever. I want them to be able to find you.

So why the long commercial? Think about it for a moment. Where are the Alliance's target audiences? Reading this book, of course! Enough said.

Your Website

There is much to know about developing a website that will serve you well and be found by your target audiences. Please don't balk, fearing it will be a technical discussion, or that somehow you'll need to learn to write HTML code. Nobody asks you to run the printing presses for the newspaper, or upload your TV commercial to the satellite, and I'm not going to suggest you need to do the actual programming of your website either.

But there is some inside information that can serve you well – information that you won't find in most marketing books but that you can discuss with your site programmer to maximize the utility of your site.

Your URL is your website address. URL = Uniform Resource Locator (just in case you're ever on Jeopardy!) and it simply refers to the fact that anyone typing your address into a web browser, uniformly, located anywhere in the world, will come up with your website.

Consider what your URL will be if you haven't yet named your business. If you want to check availability, go to a registration website like GoDaddy.com or Register.com. Type in your choice of URL, and it will tell you whether it's available. You can't tell availability from typing a URL into a browser. There are millions of already-registered URLs that don't have sites associated with them.

Your URL should represent your business without being too weird. Make sure you write it out to be sure it looks right, too. Just like you have to be careful about naming your child (Anna Susan Smith would spend her life coping with very strange initials!), you need to be careful with your URL, too.

By the way, there is no reason why you can't use capital letters when you write or type it. Look back at how I wrote www.AdvoConnection.com. Those capital letters make no difference to the browser when it goes looking for your URL, but it can make a big difference in how your target audiences read it. In particular it can make a difference if the words in your company name begin or end with vowels or with the same letter.

iowaadvocates.com is much more difficult to read than IowaAdvocates.com

insuranceeagles.com is more difficult to read than InsuranceEagles.com

advocatesservices.com is more difficult to read than AdvocatesServices.com plus people might fail to put two S's in the middle unless it's clear

One other consideration for your URL, and that is, make sure you register other possibilities that people might mistakenly think is correct. For example, if your company is Best Advocates, then register BestAdvocate.com plus BestAdvocates.com, Best-Advocate.com and Best-Advocates.com. Also consider registering the .org and .net and .us versions, too. Each year new extensions (like .ws, .info, etc) are made available, but I don't think you need to chase them all. If you are in Canada, and want to be recognized as Canadian, you seem to be stuck with .ca, likewise with .uk in Great Britain, or .au in Australia, although you could probably register some of the others, too.

Why register all those other possibilities? Because you don't want someone else squatting on your name, and potentially taking away your business. If you are BestAdvocate.com and your competition registers and uses BestAdvocates.com, you will lose business.

Ask your web developer to "alias" all those other names. That means that if anyone inputs any of your registered URLs into a browser, they will all take you to your website.

URL registration is not expensive. Each one should cost you no more than $10 or $15 a year, depending on the registrar. You'll need to renew annually (although you can get discounts if you register for five years or more at once.) Find a list of registrars in the Resources section at the end of this book.

What Information Needs to Be On Your Website?

The answer to this question is really quite simple. You need just enough to make someone contact you, and not so much they will dismiss you (see Best Practice #10 on page 51.) Of course, the devil is in the details.

When it comes to professional services websites, in particular for small businesses, I believe the simpler the better. If it's too complicated, you run the risk of confusing potential clients and perhaps even worse, failing to keep it updated.   If you can fit all this on one page without making it too busy, then sure—do it.

Here are the minimum content requirements for your site – the bare bones you need to have to be sure you can entice potential clients:

- **Name of your company**

- **Location of your company**, along with a statement of the geography you work in, such as "Providing Services Across Northern Indiana" or "Covering Connecticut"

- If you are a one or two person business, you need **photos*** of each. If you have more advocates than that, then a more generic photo of the kind of work you do is acceptable. Remember, you want to make this personal, you want people to relate. They will relate to kind faces, and to photos of someone who represents them.

  *Important: a photo of an advocate should be YOUR photo, and not some generic unknown face. Advocacy is very personal, not unlike online dating. When you meet the potential client in person, they will expect to see the face they saw online, and they will be thrown off if they don't. Be authentically you.

- **Statement of your work** – using your messages developed in Chapter Three. Bullet points are best. Make sure you list benefits above services so site visitors see themselves first.

- Your **call to action**: call us today, register for our newsletter, check our availability or another

- **Contact information** – both email and phone – on every page! Not just a link to a "CONTACT US" page, but contact information everywhere. (Nothing drives me crazier than to find only a form I need to fill out in order to contact someone, with no one managing my expectations about when I'll hear back. Email and phone seem like a short cut compared to a form. The whole point to your website is to get people to contact you. Why would you delay that?)

Also good to have:

- **Testimonials** – this will be your web approach to word-of-mouth. And just like we discussed in Chapter Seven, you will have retrieved these from satisfied clients, so they should be easy to replace on occasion.

- A **News** page – Not health news, rather news about you and your company. If you develop a media-recognized expertise (see Public Relations, Chapter Eight) then you'll want to link to any online mentions of that expertise.

- Your **Press Kit**. In Chapter Eight, we talked about press kits – information the media may want from you when they are ready to interview you. You need only a simple one, consisting of a bio / resume, a high resolution photo, some Frequently Asked Questions, and maybe some talking points. I've got a press kit on one of my sites – simple and all I've ever needed. http://youbetyourlifebooks.com/media/

- A **way to collect email addresses** (see the next bullet)....

- **Newsletter or tips** you will send out on occasion using those email addresses you have collected. (See Public Relations, Chapter Eight) You can keep copies of the ones you have already shared on your site.

- A **Sitemap** – which you'll want for Search Engine Optimization (see section coming up on SEO) Even though your site won't be extensive, this will be a page of links that search engines can "crawl" (meaning, they pick up all the links and keep looking at more pages on your site.) The more time search engines spend on your site, the better, so if you have more than three or four pages on your website, then add a Sitemap page, too.

Here's the sitemap page from one of my websites to give you an idea of how simple they can be.
www.EveryPatientsAdvocate.com/sitemap.htm

Building Your Website

The big question for some people is whether they should attempt to build their websites themselves, or pay someone else, or hire their geeky 15-year old nephew who already built one about his X-Box experiences, and pay him under the table.

If those are your choices, then I can't speak for the abilities of your 15-year-old, but I can provide some other ideas for you.

If you enjoy fooling around with computer applications, and get a kick out of figuring out how to place graphics on a page so it looks balanced, then you can give it a try yourself. Some blog software, which is free, can be used to build a webpage. Other programs are "plug and play" meaning, they have a template, and you put components into the templates. Like doing a jigsaw puzzle, or even like scrapbooking (which my sister tells me is all the rage), building a website can be challenging, but fun. Find a list of web building tools in the Resources at the back of this book.

Alternatively, you can hire someone who knows what they are doing to build one for you. The cost will range from less than $200 to $5,000 and more, depending on how extensive your site will be. The major advantage to hiring someone is that you can forego the learning curve. And as you get started in a new business, or as you grow your current business, you don't really have a lot of time for a learning curve.

In addition, there is some "backend" that takes place with a website. You'll need to register the URL you chose, you'll need to make sure it points to your new site, and you'll need to prep your site for search engines (see SEO in the next section.)

Whether you build it yourself, or you hire someone, here are some parameters you'll want to attend to, in order to make sure your site works well for your marketing:

- **Branding**. Make sure the graphic appearance and messages adhere to your brand. It's easy to get carried away with colors and elements on a website! But you'll clutter, confuse and violate your brand. Don't go there.

- **The Two Click Rule** (formerly the Three Click Rule). We web information seekers are lazy. And we are lazier today, or perhaps more impatient, than we were just a few years ago. We don't want to have to click to any more pages than we absolutely have to. Keep that in mind as you build your site. Don't make someone click, then click again, then click again to get to the information they need. Use the KISS rule. (Keep It Simple Silly!)

- **Keep your site current**. For many advocates this won't be a problem. If you don't date material, or if it's not built on a blog site, then there won't be reasons for it to look outdated. Visitors will be frustrated if they see that you site was copyrighted in 2008, for example. It just looks like nobody is paying attention. If you decide to include a news page on your site, keeping it current will be essential.

- Finally, one of the most important parts of building an effective website is optimizing it so it will **rank as high as possible in search engines**. That requires SEO.

SEO = Search Engine Optimization

Have you ever wondered how some organizations always seem to come up on the first page of results in a search engine like Google, Bing or Yahoo, while others – even though they may actually be better choices and more relevant – are nowhere in sight, perhaps positioned on the 57th page of results?

The answer is that those sites are near the top of the list because someone has optimized them to be there. Whoever built them knew how to make sure search engines move them closer to the top of the list – they optimized those sites for search engines. And of course, being at the top of the list is the goal – the brass ring for websites.

SEO is more art than science. The problem is that each of those search engines has diabolical and revengeful nerds behind it switching up the rules every day! What might work to move your site to the top of the list today will be tomorrow's reason to send you to the search engine basement. Those nerds revel in the fact that we don't know their new rules. In fact, they work hard to be sure no one can figure them out, and if they suspect that some soul has figured out how to make their site be found more quickly, they pull the plug and change the rules again.

Because SEO is such a moving target, entire companies exist that do nothing but help large websites rise in searches. They charge thousands of dollars – a month! – to do so. Our smaller businesses just can't compete. But the truth is, we don't really need to either. There aren't large corporations that do patient advocacy work (yet!) so we just need to do our best and adhere to some basic guidelines that will actually work pretty well for us.

Whether you build your own website, or work with someone else to do it, you should be aware of some of those basic guidelines to give you the best chance of being found by a potential client who does a search to find you, a patient advocate in his or her location.

We'll begin with metadata (also known as metatags.)

Behind your site is a lot of computer code called HTML (hypertext markup language) that tells your computer or browser what to do. Inside that code, mostly hidden from us, is metadata, which is where a search engine goes to learn about your website. You can add words to the metadata that will help Google, Bing, Yahoo and all other search engines know where to categorize you.

Let's take a look at some of this metadata.

Go to your computer and open your favorite web browser (Internet Explorer, Firefox, Safari or another.) Choose your favorite search engine, then search for topics using your own keywords, such as "patient advocate," "midwife," "doula," "weight loss coach," or whatever is relevant to you. Also include your location (city and state). Hit SUBMIT.

At the top of the page, you will see ads that people have paid for. (We looked at these in Chapter Nine.) For the moment, we're going to ignore them and look at the next results. Pick any of the links from the first page and link to it (Although, avoid results that may be directories. You're looking for a site that might be for someone with a business like yours.)

Once you get to that site's results (it might be their homepage, it might not), right click your mouse on a PC (or Control-Click your Mac mouse) – and your browser will produce a menu. One the menu somewhere, it will say SOURCE or PAGE SOURCE or VIEW SOURCE. Choose that. A box full of text and coding will open.

Somewhere in the top half of that text page, you will see

> META NAME = TITLE
> META NAME = DESCRIPTION

There may be some additional metadata, too[10], or one of those may be missing. These are the instructions for search engines – the information that tells them what to expect on that web page.

The idea behind metadata is to make sure it is very relevant to your page, and is loaded with the keywords your potential clients will use to find you. Notice – I didn't say words that necessarily describe your business. I said the words your potential clients will use. Put yourself in their shoes – how would you search for you? (This is the list of keywords you developed in Chapter Three – Strategy and Messages.) Your title and description must use those words, and your content, the text on the page, must use them, too. Also, if you have more than one page, then try to use different metadata for each page.

Here are some examples for the homepage of a doula who works in the Seattle area.

> <META NAME = TITLE Content = "Doulas Are Us–Childbirth Services in Seattle, Washington">
> <META NAME = DESCRIPTION Content = "Doulas Are Us provides childbirth services and birthing education in Seattle, Washington and surrounding areas.">

The last important aspect to SEO is to be sure the words you have used in your metadata show up on the webpages they are assigned to. If you're a doula, you're probably wondering why I would include Lamaze – it's not the same thing, right? Aha... but remember, you are trying to be found by pregnant women who are researching their options. Some of them will search for Lamaze – and it would be nice if they found you, too.

TASK #18

Write down your metadata for your homepage, even if you aren't ready to build a website. It's a great exercise for understanding what needs to be included on a webpage. TITLE, DESCRIPTION -- go for it.

....

A reminder that you can download the free companion workbook to
The Health Advocate's Marketing Handbook from
http://HealthAdvocateResources.com/HABMH

---

10   In the first edition of this book, another important form of metadata was called KEYWORDS, and I recommended your list of meta keywords needed to be included in your HTML code, too. However, since 2012, search engines no longer access meta keywords, so they are no longer a necessary part of this behind-the-scenes code.

More SEO

Search engines can't read graphics or images – they can only read text. They also can't read video or audio files (like podcasts). So another good practice is to turn your graphics, video or audio into text, too.

It's easy to tell which areas of a webpage are text vs images. Most images are obvious – photos, clip art, logos. But sometimes what appears as text is really an image, too. Here's how to tell which text is really text vs which is an image.

Notice that the text is highlighted – that means the search engine can read it.

Here the text can't be highlighted. Instead you'll see a pointing finger indicating it is an image that cannot be read by a search engine.

Every image can accept a description, called an alt-tag, when it's put into a webpage. Ask the person who builds your site to be sure that your meta description and keywords are repeated in your alt-tags, too. Alt-tags are also useful for SEO.

Web Links

Seeing a title like "Web links" makes most people think about the places on their website where they will link to other places, such as another page on their site, or even another website.

But the links that are valuable to SEO aren't those links. SEO requires many links coming TO your site – from other sites, outside of your site and unrelated to yours.

The more links that come TO your site, the more search engines consider your site to be an authority. The key, then, is to encourage as many of those kinds of links as possible. So, for example, if you start a blog, you want to be sure to link it back to your company website. If you become listed in the AdvoConnection Directory, that will create a link to your site. If you have a Facebook page, you'll link to your site. You can ask your kids to

Telling Search Engines About Your Site

If you've just completed your site, or if your site has been online for a while, but you search using your keywords, and you don't see your site in the results, then you'll want to let the search engines know your site is online. Each search engine has a link you can go to with a brief form to fill out that alerts them that it's time to "crawl" your site and add it to the list of sites for companies that do what yours does.

There are a number of companies that tell you they will submit your URL to dozens of search engines, for a fee. Forget it – it's not worth it.

Find a list of the submission pages in the Resources at the back of this book. Submit your site to all of them and those other search engines will pick up your site, too.

link their Facebook pages to your company website. In short, seek as many links TO your site as possible because search engines will give you a boost for each.

We've now covered Good Website Practices 101. As you can imagine, there is much more to know about building a successful site, but these good practices will get you discussing your site intelligently with the person who builds your site – or will give you some good background for building your own.

One last good idea, if you haven't already done it, is to let the search engines know your site is there once it's built. They may never find you unless you tell them you are there. See the sidebar with instructions.

If your site has been online for a while, and you search using your keywords, and you don't see your site in the results, then you'll want to try updating, then submitting your site, too.

Maximizing Use of the Web: Showcasing Expertise

In the first version of this book published in 2010, I mentioned a concept that was considered to be "on the horizon" called Web 3.0.

Well—we've reached the horizon.

Web 1.0 was the first iteration of use of the Internet by the masses. It was comprised of websites only, and we all "surfed the web."

Web 2.0 was the advent of social media. The big change was that everyone (and his brother) was able to participate online through Facebook, My Space, blogging, you name it. We upload and "SUBMIT" even more than we download to read or watch. Web 2.0 is about sharing: words, photos, images, video and audio.

The advance to Web 3.0 was first described by *Newsweek* Magazine in 2008 as "the return to the experts." They predicted that at some point we would begin to tire of the online free-for-all social media offers, and that we would, instead, begin looking to experts online— those people who continue to use the Internet as their road to respect and recognition.

What this means to us advocates is that we need to begin using the web to showcase our expertise. It's no longer just about showcasing our capabilities and marketing directly to our target audiences. It's about commanding respect for our knowledge, skills and abilities by building a reputation as an expert.

Share Your Expertise Through Blogging

Blogging can be a large part of your marketing strategy as long as you understand that it's time consuming, requires a bit of technical fiddling, and is always in the back of your mind once you start...

Is it worth it? I will tell you that it is the single biggest reason I have been able to make the strides in patient empowerment and advocacy I have been able to make.

Blogging is my platform for showing the world I am an expert.

Why? A number of reasons, but all of them key on the fact that it's because I was able to talk about a lot of aspects of patient empowerment and advocacy that a website just doesn't allow for. I address recent news, offer my opinions, introduce resources, highlight other empowered patients and advocates, whine and complain, rejoice – a little bit of everything.

Every post I write is full of keywords and links TO my websites. For my career, blogging has been huge.

I'm not going to suggest you start a blog. It's a personal decision. But I can tell you that blogging can be the impetus for growing your business quickly by showcasing your expertise and commanding respect for your capabilities.

Unlike the information on previous pages for building a website, I'm not going to write out instructions for starting a blog here. I've actually done that already at my About.com website. If you want to start a blog, or even grow the one you've already begun, you can find a link in Chapter Sixteen—Resources.

Commenting on Other Blogs

Whether or not you do decide to build a blog yourself, you can take advantage of other people's blogs. Get into the habit of checking in on some of the people who blog on the topics you are most interested in, those which relate to your work (like the APHA blog: www.APHABlog.com). Make a comment and use a signature that includes a link back to your website or to your blog.

If you don't know whose blogs to follow, set up news alerts (see Chapter Eight) using your keywords, and check off that you'd like to be notified of blogs as well as news. If those blogs get delivered as results to you, then they are being delivered to others, too. So those are the ones you want to comment on.

Also, you can do a search for "most influential health bloggers" or "top breast cancer bloggers" or whatever your interest is. Many organizations put out lists such as these and you're bound to find them with that kind of search.

Of course, if you really get active in the blogging world, maybe you'll end up on one of those lists one day yourself.

Social Networking – the Online Version of Word of Mouth

Social networking is a mystery to some, a God-send to others, and a real time-sucker for many. But when managed properly, social networking can be a huge boon to your marketing and promotion.

What's the Difference Between Social Networking and Social Media?

This is one of the silliest arguments I hear – people who have nothing better to do, spend time arguing about the differences between social media and social networking.

The truth is, there is a difference. One is a noun, the other a verb. Social media are the equipment and applications that help you do the social networking! Social media might be Twitter, Facebook, YouTube, Flikr, or IMs (instant messaging) – or your smartphone or PC where you install and use those applications.

Social networking is what you do with them. You share – through conversations, videos, podcasts, photos, links – and you share them via social media. The sharing itself – reaching out to others – is social networking.

But the two terms are often used interchangeably. As long as everyone understands what you're talking about, go ahead and use whichever term you like. Don't sweat the difference.

Suppose you had an opportunity to spend some time every day at in a coffeehouse, sipping your mocha latte, munching on some biscotti, and having random conversations with some friends, and some strangers, too. You could discuss the things you have in common, the events of your life, the good, the bad and yes, the ugly, too.

Now suppose you had that opportunity every day with people who came specifically to YOUR coffeehouse, because they needed the kind of help you could give them. They want to sit next to you, get to know you, pick your brain – and learn to trust you. And then, they hire you.

Contrast that with sitting by your telephone and waiting for it to ring. Or building a website or balancing your checkbook.

Which would you rather do? And which way will you be able to attract new clients more effectively?

Social networking is a lot like that coffeehouse – except you supply your own coffee and snacks and save the $6.50 (plus tax) for the mocha latte and biscotti.

The key is to find the right coffeehouse – where the people you'd like to meet go, and where the people you meet will be influenced, and will appreciate your expertise.

The right coffeehouse may not be the same for everyone, plus people change coffeehouses all the time. Social networking is dynamic – but that's actually part of the fun.

What coffee houses can you choose from? I can give you answers for today – but tomorrow there may be new ones we haven't heard of yet. If I had written this book in 2008, Twitter would barely have been on my radar, and Facebook was mostly populated by college kids. Today those coffee houses actually have different kinds of patrons, and new coffeehouses like Google+ and Pinterest are springing up.

Here are the most popular social media applications to choose from (as of 2014):

- FaceBook
- Google+
- Twitter
- Pinterest
- LinkedIn (and LinkedIn Groups)
- Vine
- Instagram
- YouTube
- Flikr (photos)

You may find, as I do, that different audiences can be influenced in different social media locations. I find more patients (and friends and family) on Facebook. I find more of my peers, plus providers, insurers and industry people and – key – the people who hire me to speak at conferences, on Twitter and Google+. Because there isn't much to photograph in patient empowerment and advocacy, I haven't spent more than a few moments with Pinterest.

Begin by choosing one of them. Learn how to use it, play with it a little, meet some new people with whom you share commonalities, and others you can learn from. Use your keywords when you set up your profiles, be sure to link to your website and your blog if you have one, and check in on your social media account consistently.

The real key to success with any of them is that they are meant to be like that coffee house – two way conversations, opportunities to share, learn and laugh.

Once you're comfortable with one, then try a second one. Some aren't so much about the conversation as they are about your expertise. Make videos for YouTube. Pin images at Pinterest. Upload photos to Flikr. The focus here is to add pieces to those which you can then promote through your blog, and link to your website. Remember – one of our marketing best practices is to make each part of your marketing refer to other parts of your marketing. Social media is prime referral real estate.

I've been involved in social networking since 2009 and I'm still learning to use it well. Further, as I said a few paragraphs ago, social media and networking are moving targets – we must make the effort to keep up with them.

Here's an invitation for you to get you started: Join Google+ and find our Patient Empowerment and Advocacy Community. Meet great people, learn from them, share your expertise with us all. It's an easy, unintimidating way to get started. We'll welcome you.

Online Support Groups

There are a number of sites that host health-related support groups. I've provided a link to a list of those I know about in the Resources chapter at the end of this book.

Like commenting on other people's blogs, participating in these support groups can be a good way to let people know you and your work can help them. At first you'll want to just read what people have to say, getting a sense of the groups' values and interests. Begin participating gradually.

Be yourself, but be protective of your personal identity, too. If someone approaches you asking you for more information about your services, then trust your gut as to whether you want to disclose any more information to them. Probably easiest to share your website's URL which will only give away public information.

Extending Your Online Reach

When you are ready to take the next marketing leaps online, meaning your website is under control, your blog is working well for you, and you've got a good handle on social media, then you might want to take advantage of some additional online opportunities.

Ever want to be a disk jockey? These days there are ways to build a following with an internet radio show. There are free and inexpensive web applications and sites that give you all the tools you need to start up a radio show where, as the good advocate you are, you can talk about health-related topics with guests who can inform your audience. You might remove the word "disk" but you can jockey your way to a nice following online through this medium.

Why not write a book? It doesn't have to be long or involved, but more and more people are writing e-books – books that might be given away for free, or sold at a low cost. E-books can be read on computers, tablets, Kindles, Nooks or iPads. Most require entirely different formatting, but entry into this form of marketing is getting easier.

Measuring Your Web Marketing Results

There are two important aspects to measuring the marketing effect of your website. You will want to measure not just how many people visit your site, but what they do once they get there.

Here's how:

As your site is being built, ask your webmaster to add "analytics" to it. There are any number of programs that will provide you with statistics, most of which are free. Some of these programs are just built into the hosting of your site. Google offers a program called "Google Analytics." There are many others.

Those statistics can tell you a great deal about who is visiting your website, when and why they decided to visit your site, and what they are doing when they get there.

The best way to learn about the information that's available through these statistics is to spend some time staring at them and figuring out how to translate them. For example, you may have an average of 25 visitors per day. But a look at your analytics tells you that 50 people visited your website between noon and 1 PM last Tuesday. And 50 more visited your site during the next few hours. It so happens that last Tuesday you were interviewed by your local noon news anchor on TV. But now you know what an effect your appearance made.

Was there a story in your local newspaper about patient advocacy? Did you speak to the members of a local church or synagogue? Check the statistics for the next 24 to 48 hours to see if your numbers went up.

Having lots of visitors is definitely a good thing. But it's even better if those visitors translate into new clients. You can help that translation by being sure you have a call to action on every one of your web pages. You'll also know if your email box filled up with new requests or your phone rang with calls from people who saw you on TV, then visited your website.

But if you know you had a lot of visitors, but you didn't get a lot of new contacts, then that tells you something else. It means you either need to tweak your messages to the benefits of working with you more clear, or you need to improve your call to action. Or, it may mean you need to make it easier to find your contact information on your website.

There's one other way to make your web visitor measurement more specific. Create a specific URL to send visitors to, for specific reasons. For example, you might speak to the Rotary Club and as a promotion, promise them a free half-hour consultation. The only way they can take advantage of that promotion is to go to this URL: www.YourWebsite.com/Rotary

Ahead of time, you'll ask your webmaster to build a page that will be there when the Rotary member who visits it that will tell them how to take advantage of the free half-hour promotion. But what it really tells you is how successful your talk at the Rotary Club was, because you'll be able to look at your statistics to figure out how many Rotarians visited your site.

On the Web Horizon...

... that I know about. As this book goes to press, I do know one thing... the "next big thing" is on the horizon – and will come out just a few days after this handbook is published. Of course, I have no idea what it might be, but that's how fast opportunities and communications on the web are multiplying.

But here are some newer technologies and topics that may, someday, be a part of your marketing through the Internet, too.

Smartphones: already many people check for webpages on their phones. Because of this, consider a "mobile" version of your website. You'll want to register the .mobi URL for your business. Ask your web developer how big a leap it would be to make a smartphone version of your website.

Tele-Advocating: You've probably heard of telemedicine – where doctors are able to help patients at rural, remote hospitals with strokes or heart attacks. With a specialized internet hookup, the doctor in a larger city hospital, who has all the equipment and capabilities, can help doctors in those remote places help their patients, stabilizing them to be transported to the larger hospital later.

So, why not tele-advocating? A consultation using Skype (a free video-teleconferencing application) would allow you to meet with your clients or potential clients conveniently – no travel. In particular, if your work is constrained by geography, tele-advocating could help you extend your reach.

No matter to what extent you decide to use the Internet for your marketing, do it now.

································

From the world of electronic messages, we'll return to the old days – for some tools we still find useful. Collateral – printed marketing materials... Yes, there is still room for them in our marketing tool arsenal.

Chapter Eleven
Tools & Tactics:
Marketing Collateral
(Printed Materials)

Tool: Collateral (Printed Materials)

Description: Printed pieces ranging from business cards to glossy multi-page booklets or brochures.

Pros: Branded perfectly, controlled messages, can be developed for your specific target audiences.

Cons: Once printed, not easy to make changes, can be expensive, may be difficult to distribute

When used in marketing-speak, collateral refers to printed matter you might give potential clients or influencers to share your expertise or convince them to hire you.

Here is a list of collateral pieces you could develop:

- Business cards
- Brochures and Flyers
- FAQs—Frequently Asked Questions
- Testimonials printed as a one-page flyer, branded
- White papers—authoritative guides on issues your work focuses on
- Company Backgrounder—people, history, philosophy and more

For many businesses, collateral seems so... yesterday! But for many health advocates, particularly those who work with older patients, the opposite is probably true – at least for another ten years.

Older patients who don't use the Internet, and others who don't have easy access to the Internet, don't have efficient ways to get information about you. To reach out to them, you may need printed materials and places to put them to be sure they are found.

Even advocates who can do outreach online may find printed materials useful. For example, if you provide hospital bedside services, a supply of brochures in your briefcase can be a simple and convenient response to anyone who asks who you are while you perform your duties. How convenient when the family of the person in the next bed is getting frustrated with their loved one's care!

If the bulk of your advocacy work is more focused on younger, web-accessing people, then you may not need as many brochures as your compatriots who work with an older population. On the other hand, it's easy to carry them with you no matter where you go. Just because people have access to the Internet at home or work doesn't mean they have access as they ride the subway, attend Lamaze class, pick up their kids at daycare, or work out in the gym.

Business cards are a must – and you give them to everyone for every reason. Don't fill them with too much information (the less said, the more read, remember?) but make sure you have a statement of exactly what you do.

Brochures, branded well and printed professionally can be great handouts to accompany your business cards. Flyers,can also be used as small posters which can be hung on bulletin boards in churches or daycare centers, gyms or even supermarkets.

The other pieces of collateral on the list may come in handy at some point, especially if you decide to develop a printed media kit, which we covered in Chapter Eight.

What Information Belongs in Your Collateral?

Here are some specifics to keep in mind as you plan for the content of your printed materials.

- Your printed materials need to be about your target audiences – not you. Find the notes you made about your target audiences in Chapter Two.
- Your printed materials need to include your messages: your services and benefits, your unique selling proposition and your positioning statement—those you developed in Chapter Three.
- Your brochure needs to reflect your branding.
- Make sure all collateral adheres to the best practices outlined in Chapter Five.

Simple, right? OK, maybe not. But you have already developed all the content you need for your collateral as you developed your strategy, and you know what the best practices are. You might be thinking it was easier before you knew all that. But the truth is – easier does not equal effective. With all your background, you are in a position to create collateral that will actually work for you.

Get Creative

By creative, I don't mean you need to go wild with colors and fonts–that would violate your branding! But creativity can help you tailor your materials to your audience.

For example, you might have several versions of your brochure to use for different audiences. If part of your audience is older cancer patients, then you will want to develop a different brochure for the parents of children with cancer.

You may want to develop a smaller marketing piece – not a full blown brochure or even an event flyer – that addresses one simple thing. I give bookmarks to people to promote my first book, *You Bet Your Life! The 10 Mistakes Every Patient Makes (How to Fix Them to Get the Health Care You Deserve).* It has only the book cover, a one-sentence positioning statement about the content of the book, and the web address (along with the call-to-action – Buy this book!) That's it! I carry them in my purse and briefcase, and give away 10-12 a week.

You can use such a tailored piece when a business card isn't exactly right, and you to include a call to action. A hospital bedside advocate might use something simple like, "Having challenges getting the attention you need? Call a patient advocate." Then include your phone number. Or a weight loss coach might make up a postcard with a caricature of a heavy person with a question like, "Can't do it alone? Joe Henderson will help you get rid of those extra pounds." Again – don't forget the call to action and the contact information.

Who Should Develop Your Collateral?

Deciding who should develop your brochure or other printed pieces depends on your ability to use design and layout computer software and your budget.

Part of your answer will depend on who you will be giving your brochure to. If you live and work in an area that has become somewhat sophisticated in its understanding of health advocates, then you may need a more sophisticated or professional brochure. On the other hand, if you are the only act in a 100-mile radius, then maybe not.

Your brochure should reflect your approach to your work, too. If you command very high prices for your work, your brochure needs to look like you are worthy of all that money.

You may decide to work with a graphic artist, perhaps the person who has developed the graphic representation of your brand. If so, you'll want to use the information in this book to guide the content. If that's the case, then just like you asked friends and former clients to review your messages, you might ask them to review your brochure, too, to see if it answers the questions they might have about your services.

If you decide to turn the entire project over to professionals, then they will ask you to help them develop the content that should be included in your brochure. You'll already be way ahead of the game, having already developed that information during Chapter Three. If they don't ask you, then that may be a red flag about working with them. At the very least, you'll have something to compare it to, knowing now what information belongs in it.

What About Printing?

Unless you have just been invited to speak to more than 500 people, then don't print more then a few hundred brochures for your first printing. There are a couple of reasons for this:

First, depending on your target audience and your opportunities to reach out to them, you may not have too many times you can actually give brochures away to people.

Second, I can almost guarantee that as soon as you've printed them, you'll think of something you wish was different – or – within a few months, something will have changed in your business, and it will require a change to your brochure, too.

Don't forget, you can also make your brochure available on your website. People can request you mail a copy to them – or better yet – let them print it themselves from your site, perhaps from your Media Kit section. Plus, by including your brochure online, it's fairly easy to make those updates and edits that may be needed.

Other Collateral Tools and Tactics

This is by no means a comprehensive list of marketing collateral tools and tactics. They are just the ones you will likely want to use as a health advocate.

If you find or develop additional materials, I'd love to hear about them.

A Note About Your Business Forms

Marketing collateral and business forms are really two different things with two different purposes. Your forms are used to gather information about clients or potential clients whereas your collateral pieces are used to provide information to those clients. But that doesn't mean you can't make your forms do a bit of marketing for you, too.

If you have forms that clients actually fill out themselves (not those you will fill out as you have a conversation with them), then you might want to include your logo and contact information to make it easy for them to contact you if they have questions. Particularly if they will fill out those forms when you aren't around—the easier you make it for them to contact you with questions, the better sense they will have that you make their lives easier. That's a great impression for an advocate to leave.

The Marketing Collateral Bottom Line

Collateral – printed marketing pieces – can be anything you want them to be to fill a void in the information you have. They can be any size, any color, for any purpose. I've given you examples here, but you can get as creative as you want to. The only thing I ask is that you double check that you always – ALWAYS – have your call-to-action and contact information printed, clearly. Because contacting you is the entire point of creating and distributing collateral.

Chapter Twelve
Miscellaneous Tools & Tactics

Marketing advice often varies in its recommendations of tools and tactics, even for helping professions like health advocacy.

The basics are the same. New, creative ideas pop up frequently. The ability to market on the web is evolving, but even those tactics are simply rewoven from other tactics, and tailored for use on the web.

But mostly, the basics are the basics. You'll find only some slight disagreements in the ways they get categorized. For example, one marketing resource will consider a postal-mailed newsletter to be public relations. Online, you might find reference to developing a newsletter – but it, of course, is referring to a newsletter you would send by email. Or is a newsletter advertising? It might be, depending on its content. Still others would call a newsletter "direct mail" which is another category of marketing we haven't yet covered. You can see what I mean by "rewoven."

So here is a list of some miscellaneous ideas. Each might have been included in another, labeled chapter of this book. But I want you to get the sense that marketing is more about creativity – perhaps not so much about being correctly labeled, or following 'the rules."

Customer Service

One unique aspect to customer service is that not all marketers even agree that it should be considered marketing at all! However, I consider it to be adjunct to word-of-mouth. As such, it becomes very important to our marketing.

Customer service goes hand-in-hand with managing expectations, too. You know this from your own experiences (and our earlier example of what happens when you try to use a coupon in the store when they are all out of the advertised products.) The better you manage expectations among your target audiences and influencers, the better served they will feel.

...which will then translate to great testimonials once you've finished your work with them, which can be used in your marketing materials, etc etc....

The ripple effect of good customer service can be enormous – both positively and negatively.

Customer service can make or break your marketing, just as word-of-mouth can. Unfortunately, it's easier to flip to the negative side than you can imagine. Many moons ago, I was the marketing director at my local community college. We spent hundreds of thousands of dollars each year enticing students to attend our college. Then the security guys began putting $5 parking tickets on the cars parked adjacent to the Admissions building -- which drove potential students away.

Lousy customer service is like shooting yourself in the foot.

Treat your clients like the gold they are. Manage their expectations, under-promise and over-deliver. In short, understand that you can enhance or destroy your marketing though customer service—or non-service.

Direct Mail ("Junk Mail")

Every day I go out to my mailbox at the end of my driveway, pull the mail from the box, and walk back through my garage, often dropping more than half of that mail into my recycling bin. It's junk.

That's how most of us regard direct mail – as junk mail. Which is why I haven't spent a lot of time on it in this book.

However, we shouldn't just dismiss direct mail. IF it is well-targeted and IF it is timely, then it's really a great tool for reaching our target audience. The problem is those two big IFs.

If you could deliver a marketing postcard or letter to

- a patient, or the caregiver for a patient

- who could use and afford your services

- within hours of they became fearful or frustrated enough to contact you

… then direct mail would be a great way to reach out to them.

But now you see the challenges. The success of direct mail is tied to pinpointing target audiences and timing. Just as we did the math to figure out if advertising would be worth it (see Chapter Nine), we would need to do the math to make that same determination for direct mail. The variables for direct mail are a bit different – you'd have to factor in printing and postage, plus your conversation rates are typically lower than they are in other forms of advertising.

But if they hit the mark, they can be very profitable.

If you are interested in trying some direct mail, then it will be worth your while to contact someone who understands the many aspects and best practices for direct mail marketing. You want to be sure you are spending your money efficiently, in ways you can measure well.

Promotions

Everyone likes to think they are getting more than they paid for, or something for free. For many products and services, promotions might include contests or coupons – even buy-one-get-one-free.

Unfortunately, those don't really lend themselves well to many types of health advocacy (which is one reason Promotions have ended up in our Miscellaneous Chapter.) If they aren't done right, health advocacy promotions can have the effect of cheapening your service – making it seem less professional.

If you are a strength trainer, or a massage therapist, you might consider a promotion that would allow someone a free visit – that would be promotional and wouldn't violate anyone's ideas of professionalism.

Those who work on the patient advocacy side of this business might consider promotional tactics like reducing the price of a health assessment (be sure you make it known how rarely you reduce that price in your marketing.) Or promote the idea of providing a 20-minute phone assessment for free.

Another promotion might be based on referrals. If a patient or caregiver refers a friend to you, and the friend hires you, you might give the referrer a gift card or pay for their dinner in a nice restaurant.

Be imaginative with promotions. But be sure to manage expectations in the process, too. Make your 'rules' very clear, and don't give away so much that you dilute the perception of your services or expertise at other times.

Contests or Drawings

Similar to promotions, holding a drawing is a great way to give the perception that someone is winning something, or getting more than they paid for, or something for free.

If you give talks about your services, ask people to provide their names, phone numbers and email addresses on sheets of paper attached to a clipboard (which can make the rounds while you talk) or on slips of paper as they enter the room where you'll be speaking.

At the end of your presentation, draw one of the names (or choose the 15th one on the list) and give them something tangible OR an entré to one of your services. You might give them a free health assessment. Or you might give them a book or a gift card, or a free coaching session.

You can then use those names and email addresses in your marketing. You can add them to your email list for your newsletter, or you can follow up the talk with an email to everyone in the group that shares some of the tidbits you provided during the presentation – plus a link to your website.

Tradeshows

There are fairs, conferences and tradeshows taking place year round for your target audiences. Baby fairs, senior fairs, health fairs – you name it, your target audiences and influencers are there – making it very easy to reach out to them in person.

Set up a booth, purchase a nice sign to hang in front or behind your table. Give out brochures, and some sort of tschatchke (pens, pencils, notepads, anything with your logo and phone number on it.) Engage as many people as possible in conversation.

Collect names and contact information for a drawing. Be sure to provide some kind of food (candy, or a snack of some sort.) There's some statistic on the numbers of people who will simply walk by a booth that has no food – and the numbers that flock to a table where treats are available. It's definitely worth it to have munchies available.

Have someone take a photo of you standing in front of your booth, perhaps with a show visitor, making sure your logo shows up in the photo – and put it on your website. I can't tell you why, but there seems to be some credibility associated with such a photo. Perhaps it makes you seem more like a real person to your potential clients.

Gifts

By mentioning gifts, I'm not referring to gifts like the promotional giveaways or drawings mentioned earlier. In this case, I mean giving gifts, perhaps during holiday time, to your clients. It doesn't have to be something elaborate, nor expensive. There may be some constraints (beyond the cost to you) – for example, you shouldn't give candied popcorn to your patient who is diabetic. But consider holiday or special foods. Or fruit baskets. Perhaps the legendary fruitcake! Or something fun like movie tickets or something you've chosen with your individual client in mind.

Birthdays, end of the year holidays, contract coming to a close... Everyone loves a gift, and loves to be remembered.

Or (yes, another shameless plug) I have a great book for patients available at a discount. You'll find more information in Chapter Sixteen—Resources.

Surveys

One of the oft-repeated maxims in this book is to ask for feedback from your clients. Surveys are one way to do that, a way that also allows you to add a marketing twist.

When you ask for feedback, you can frame the questions in such a way as to be marketing at the same time. Here are some examples:

Question:

Of the many services Miss Advocate provided to you, which did you appreciate the most? (Fill in the blank.)

Which were less valuable to you? (Fill in the blank.)

By using a survey, you can ask these questions differently, outlining the services in a marketing framework. It reminds people of everything you have done for them, and forces them to give some additional thought to the relationship. It also provides you with some great feedback on the value of each of your services. See if this sounds more like marketing:

Question: Please rate the following on a scale of 1 to 5 (1 being the least value, 5 being the most):

- Your initial assessment and health report
- Your weekly telephone update
- Having a companion in the doctor's office who recorded your visit
- Your medication review for potential conflicts

Presented this way, you have the opportunity to remind your client of the many services you provided, and the benefits to them. They are far more likely to be appreciative and to say nice things.

Further, if you give them an option for NA (not applicable) then you can list everything you do on the survey. If they didn't avail themselves of that service, they can check off the NA, but it's a clear reminder that you do provide that service if they ever feel the need to hire you for additional assistance.

Surveys can be presented on paper (include a self-addressed stamped envelope for return) or online using one of a number of free applications (see Chapter Sixteen—Resources.) If you provide different kinds of advocacy services, you can develop as many surveys as you care to so that those who only took advantage of a few of your services won't have to slog through too many questions that don't apply. Of course, the more they run into questions that don't apply, the less likely they are to complete your survey.

The Yellow Pages

There is a reason the Yellow Pages have gotten thinner and thinner. Because everyone is now online.

Unless "everyone" turns out to be one of your clients who doesn't go online.

You know your target audiences better than anyone else. If you suspect they (as a general rule – as a group) are still using the printed Yellow Pages, then go ahead and get in touch with your local Yellow Pages representative and ask how much various ad sizes would cost. Contact information should be found right there in those Yellow Pages. If you don't have a copy, then check at your local library.

One caveat – even if you think your target audiences are still using the Yellow Pages, you don't know for sure (yet) that they will even know to look for a patient advocate. Most areas don't even use that category in their Yellow Pages. Ask the representative where your ad would appear. You'll want to refer to your keywords from Chapter Three – because people will use those same words to look up services in the Yellow Pages, whether they are online or not.

Memberships

Your membership in some organizations, and presence at their meetings, can be a great way to market your services, particularly when you want to reach out to influencers.

Consider service and social organizations like your Chamber of Commerce, business networking groups, even the Elks or VFW, Lions or Rotary or Optimists and others.

Being on their rosters is a form of credibility because these kinds of groups provide community service. You may volunteer to speak at their meetings. You'll meet good people who will be interested in the work you do, and you'll have an opportunity, in particular, to do that education component of marketing to some very influential people.

The only caveat here is that you won't want to spread yourself too thin. Begin by joining one organization at a time. Remember, the more time you spend serving their needs, the less time you have to devote to building your business.

·······························

Believe it or not, you've now made it through the vast array of marketing tools and tactics and you've learned how strategy plays such an important role.

Now it's time to begin putting it all together into a real marketing plan for you and your business.

Chapter Thirteen
Building Your Marketing Plan

And now we get down to the real brass tacks. It's been a long, slow and information-packed wind-up. Let's hurl this one across home plate. (Always wanted to use a real sports metaphor.) Let's build your marketing plan.

Truth be told, if you have followed along with this book, using the downloadable handbook, and taking the tasks seriously as you've gone along, then you've already handled the difficult parts.

If You Build It...

.As a health advocate, you will benefit most from a 9-part plan which, when put together, will give you the roadmap you need to plan, execute, then review and refine your marketing. Done right and well, it will lead to successfully marketing your business.

Here's my "manage your expectations" caveat:

All you are doing here is writing things down – making a plan. It will be up to you to actually DO what you decide to do in order to make it all work. Just because you build your plan, doesn't mean it will make itself work!

Further – successful marketing is not the same as a successful business. In fact, you will learn that the more successful your marketing is, the more challenged you will be with other parts of your business. An increase in the number of clients you have, and expanding the services you provide to them, will force you to make other business decisions like bringing on more staff, or finding a bookkeeper, or needing an attorney to review your contracts. Marketing and the other aspects of your business go hand-in-hand, but success in one aspect doesn't necessarily promise your business will be successful.

Now that you have the marketing plan reality check, let's begin putting your plan together.

The 9-Part Marketing Plan

The rest of this chapter will take you through all but the last of the following sections (the remaining section will be tackled in Chapter Fourteen.)

Here are the nine sections of a health advocate's marketing plan:

1. Market and Situation Analysis

2. Goal Setting – Where will your marketing plan take you?

3. Competitive Review – Who or what stands in the way of your success?

4. Target Audience Definition

5. Messaging, Including the USP

6. Defining Your Brand

7. Choosing Tools and Tactics

8. Plan Execution and Measurement

9. Review, Refine, Adjust

Note: If you haven't already done so, you'll want to download the free workbook that goes along with this handbook to complete the building of your marketing plan. (http://HealthAdvocateResources.com/HABMH)

As you fill in each section, do your best to keep it simple. This is not intended to be a lifelong assignment that you'll never finish. It's intended to be an outline of a roadmap. Someday you may need to adjust your route or fix a flat – but you'll get there, and you'll be better able to do that if you keep the answers in this original document fairly simple.

Section 1. Market and Situation Analysis

There are three parts of this first section.

Part I: Research

Very formal marketing plans require you to do some major market research to build this first section – the market analysis. They require you to do phone interviews or direct mail surveys or other forms of data building and analysis to arrive at an answer to these questions.

The point to market research is to determine whether your service is needed, and whether people will hire you to do it, whether there is already too much competition in your marketplace, and therefore, whether you have a viable idea for a business.

Here's the problem for advocates. We're too new.

Since so few people know what a private health advocate does, or how working with one can benefit them, or even realize they would need to pay for the service, it's almost impossible to get useful results by doing standard marketing research.

There are some exceptions. If you are a doula or a midwife, for example, you can do some research to learn how many women of child-bearing years there are, located in your geography, who make enough money to hire you. Most of this information is available online. You may have to do some math, but you can arrive at some numbers that may convince you that building your birthing business is a good idea – or you may decide there are just too many available in your area already and you need to do something else. Most of this information is available from the US Census Bureau.[10]

However, for most health advocates, those who will need to do much of their marketing in the education mode we reviewed in Chapter Two, we have to take some leaps of faith.

If you did a survey of a random group of adults, you would find that the majority of them have some sort of health or health cost challenge. Further, they would tell you they aren't getting the help they need from the healthcare system. Therefore, no matter what kind of assistance you provide, you will find an audience.

So, while the purists are baring their teeth at me for saying this, I'm suggesting you can skip the expensive interviews and surveys and answer these questions based on your common sense and some digging on the Internet:

Part II:

Answer the following, using the notes from the tasks you did in the strategy chapters of this book:

- Who needs your services? (Not much detail needed, like you needed for describing your target audiences; rather something simple like "patients with terminal diseases" or "pregnant women". Also, do not include influencers here – only those who you will actually attend to.)

- Of 100 people, how many of them might need help at any given moment? (A guesstimate, yes, but you know your audiences well enough to make it an educated one.)

- What special requirements do you have for these clients? (Examples: they must be willing to pay for your services, they must live in the United States, etc.)

- Where are they located? (Examples: within a 100 mile radius of your city, or throughout Canada)

- Why will they want to hire you? (Again, keep this simple. You'll have an opportunity to elaborate later.)

---

10   http://quickfacts.census.gov/qfd/index.html

- What do they do now to get these services? (Examples: currently being cared for by their also elderly spouses, or being attended by ob-gyns. Simplicity here – you'll be describing competition in more detail later.)

- How can you change their current access and opportunities? (Example: building your health advocacy business to provide them with new options and better outcomes.)

- What specific opportunities will you be able to capitalize on? Are there new trends that can boost your business? (Healthcare reform might be considered an opportunity. Swine flu was one in 2009. Can you think of others?)

- What threats might get in your way? Are there roadblocks to your success? (If you do hospital billing reviews, and the United States switches to universal, totally government-sponsored care, then you would be out of business. That said, don't hold your breath. Instead, think of other possible threats such as three other advocates going into business doing exactly the work you do, within your geographic territory.)

Part III:

Now answer these questions based on your own math and knowledge of your business:

- How many clients do you already have who are paying you to do your advocacy work?

- How many clients do you need to make your business viable into the future?

- Do you already have the capability to offer your entire list of services, or do you need new training or credentials to do your work?

- How many people will be working directly with patients/clients and will be getting paychecks for doing so? (This will help you determine how much business you need to bring in.)

Section 2. Setting Your Marketing Goals

Your situation analysis was where you are, and what your marketplace looks like. Now we need to figure out where you want to be – what you are aiming for.

Your marketing plan is being built to bridge the gap between your current situation and where you want to be.

Some of you will be able to breeze through this section of your business plan. You know just where you want to go with your new advocacy work. You may have already decided that you'll forever be a one-person business. Or maybe your plan is to grow your company by adding many more advocates and expanding your outreach or the services you offer.

No matter what direction you want to take your company eventually, I have two pieces of advice for you when it comes to goal setting:

Dream big! But don't set yourself up for failure. If you try to grow your business too fast, or you try to bite off more marketing tasks that you can chew (time or cost) then you will likely neglect important tasks, creating a bigger problem for yourself than if you take a more measured approach.

Some of your goals will be about the actual building of your business and marketing (I will complete my first website by month 4.) Others will be about your growth (I will increase my number of patients by 20% by the end of year 1.)

Even in the midst of dreaming big, be conservative in your approach. For example, you may hope to expand to offer services across the United States one day. That's definitely dreaming big. One advocate might define that as a goal within three years. Another might be more conservative by planning to cover the U.S. within ten years.

In Chapter Fourteen, we'll cover the next step in marketing planning; that is, how to review and refine your plan. You'll learn that you'll be reviewing your plan at measured intervals. Each time you review and refine, you'll have the opportunity to revise goal dates, too. You'll see that it's much easier and more satisfying to shorten time frames or adjust for increased business than it is to have to take steps backwards because you've been too aggressive in your planning at the beginning.

So let's begin our goal setting.

- Begin by choosing time frames, such as: six months, one year, three years, five years There are two purposes for these time frames. One is to make sure you are building gradually, and these time frames will give you a progressive view of what you need to accomplish. The second reason is that you'll need to review your plan occasionally. We'll review this more in Chapter Fourteen.

- For each of those time periods, describe:

- How many clients (total) you hope to have and/or how many different services you'll be performing for those clients (remember – your business can expand by having more clients or offering more services.)

- How many of those clients will be the same ones you already have?

- How many clients will you lose (because your work is finished, because they die, because they move away) and have to replace?

- How many of those clients will be new – as a result of your marketing efforts?

- Will you expand your services? And how will that relate to the clients described above?

- What additional marketing will you have to do to maintain your current workload, or achieve this growth?

- What other business decisions will you need to make if you choose to grow? (Example: if you decide to double your number of clients, you won't be able to double the time you have in any given day to work with them. So how will you manage that increased business?)

Section 3: Who is Your Competition?

We discussed competition vs coopetition in Chapter Two. It's a good idea to review that right now before you fill in this next section...

(tap... tap... tap...) Finished? OK. Let's move on.

Regardless of who is competition vs. coopetition, there are some competitors who will be obvious to you, and others you've not thought about in quite that way.

What you want to list in this area is all those businesses and non-businesses that get in the way of someone paying you to do the work you do. By that definition, I suppose you could say that someone's good health becomes competition! But that's not it exactly either.

Are there other advocates who compete with you in your service area, offering the exact same services? (This will help you understand why we developed your USP in Chapter Three.) If so, list some of them and why you consider them directly competitive.

Are there other advocates who offer similar services even if they aren't exactly the same? If so, list them, and the similarities and differences from your business.

Now expand your definition of competition to other people who offer the services you offer who don't consider themselves to be health advocates, per se. (Examples: physicians and nurse practitioners, practicing in a medical office, might be competitors. Or a home health service might be willing to accompany a patient to a doctor's appointment. Or a CPA or bookkeeper might be willing to review someone's hospital bills. Or a local gym might have a coach, even if that coach doesn't focus on heart patients.)

Expand your definition even further to anything at all that competes for the money someone might pay you. For example, an adult child of an elderly, failing parent might choose to move his parent into a nursing home rather than hire an advocate who might offer enough services so she could stay home (Remember Mrs. Franklin in Chapter Two?).

One form of competition isn't exactly that, but belongs here. That is – the general lack of knowledge about the existence of health advocates. If people don't even realize health advocates exist, they won't think to look for you. Be aware at all times that you are educating them about two things:

- What health advocates like you can do to help them, and
- What your USP is – why they should be hiring YOU among the others who do the work you do.

By listing these competitors and the reasons they are truly competition, you will have a better understanding of the objections someone might have to hiring you. You can devise answers to those objections so that when you are working to sell your services to a potential client (remember, marketing supports sales), you will know how to anticipate and answer those objections.

Section 4: Define Your Target Audiences

Remember all the people we talked about in Chapter Two? It's time to pull from your workbook notes to answer these questions:

- Who will your clients be? (the people you actually help)
- Who will pay you to provide services to your clients?
- Who can influence other people to pay you for your services?
- Will you consider media as an influencer?
- Do you have any coopetition who might be influencers? List them, and describe how you may be able to help each other.

Section 5: Your Messages: Services, Benefits, and More

Again – this should be quite easy if you performed the tasks in Chapter Three and designed your messages.

- What services will you offer?
- What benefits will your audiences find from working with you?
- What is your positioning statement? (Same as your elevator speech.)
- What is your USP?

Section 6: Define Your Brand

Go back to the discussion of branding in Chapter Four, and review your task assignments for that chapter. This section of your marketing plan will be practically fill-in-the-blank with work you have already done.

- What is your company name?
- Describe your graphic identity.
- Include a copy of your logo.
- What do you want your brand's personality to be? (Examples: fun and frisky? No, probably more like professional and high quality.)

Since we've defined your messages in Section 5 of this plan, we won't duplicate them here, even though your messages are integral to your brand and its promises.

Section 7: Choosing Your Tools and Tactics

This section will require more work than the previous parts of this marketing plan. You'll be making some choices based on what you read about the many tools and tactics available to you.

Begin by referring to the table of tools in Chapter Six. This is the broad overview of possibilities, although don't let it constrain your ideas. If you come up with something you'd like to try that's not on the list – give it a shot!

The workbook that accompanies this book (http://HealthAdvocateMarketing.com) provides you with a chart that makes it easier for you to choose your tactics. It lists all the possibilities from the table in Chapter Six. And gives you the opportunity to plan for the same four time periods you defined in your goals.

Or – you can make up your own chart. The real point is to understand your strategies, then to go through the various tactics and make an educated guess, based on all the other background work we've done here, as to which tactics you'd like to use for your marketing.

Pay special attention to the rating system on the table. For example, all advocates must have business cards and must have a website. There are other "must do" tactics, some that would be beneficial if you have time and money to afford them, and others that aren't so important, but might work in your circumstances.

Also, as you choose your tactics, make decisions about how you will measure their success. Those possibilities were discussed as each tactic was described previously in this book, but you may have additional ways you can track their success (or lack thereof.)

These first seven sections of your marketing plan all relate to how you will market. The next one is actually executing the plan itself.

Section 8: Execute Your Marketing Plan

Once you have the first parts of your plan put together, you'll be ready to put it into motion. Do what it tells you to do!

As you go through your plan, be sure to keep notes on what works the way you want it to, and what does not. Track costs, and do your best to evaluate the value of each tactic.

If you encounter new competition, or you find your messages need to be refined – take notes on those too. Any aspects of your plan are ripe for reworking – just keep a log of what works, what doesn't, and if you can figure it out, why it does or doesn't work.

Bottom line – your plan is not set in stone, it's simply a suggestion – an educated suggestion of how you can begin to achieve your goals.

■■■■■■■■■■■■■■■■■■■■■■■■■■■

Now it's time for Part 9 of your plan – making those refinements. Recalculating to make it work even better for you. And a few considerations you might not have thought about before.

Chapter Fourteen
Reviewing and Refining Your Plan

So your marketing plan is built, it's been incorporated into your business plan, and perhaps you've even begun working on some of the action steps. I hope it's been a satisfying experience so far. Most likely you are just happy to have so much of it behind you.

Whether or not you are in a business start-up mode, and particularly if you haven't begun executing your plan yet, then I suggest you take the plan you've built, and perhaps this book, to a visit with a business development advisor.

Business development services are available to small business owners to answer questions and get guidance about building a business of any kind. You've probably heard of the SBA (Small Business Administration) or SCORE (Service Corps of Retired Executives). Many states offer SBDCs (Small Business Development Centers), often located at, or accessible through community colleges or other state government business support programs. If you aren't sure what services are available to you locally, a quick call to your closest community college will refer you to the right place, even if it isn't located right there.

Most of these services are free. They are made available by federal and state governments because small businesses are the backbone of both the American and Canadian economies. By helping you build your business, they are helping you improve employment (even if it's just you!)

So, knowing these folks are available to help you, they are the perfect people to advise you on your marketing plan, and to help you review what you have built. Take advantage of their services!

Creating a Review Schedule

If you followed the instructions for building your marketing plan in Chapter Thirteen, then you determined your goals in time-frames.

One reason for a timed format is to give yourself both a long and short term view of your business.

How Long Will It Take to Know Your Business Is Successful?

Your success will be based on your goals. If you have defined success as building a business that keeps you happy, busy and off the streets, then it may not matter how much money you make, and you may be successful from day one.

However, most of us will define at least part of our success on the amount of money we are making in our business. Business advisory groups use this money measurement to help define your success, too. According to those experts, it takes between three to five years to know whether you will be able to sustain your business.

How will you know your business is financially successful? The experts look to various financial statements[11] to determine a business's success.

An example is whether or not a business is operating with a positive cash-flow over time. Cash flow means you've got enough or more money coming in from your products and services than you are spending to keep the business afloat. Salaries and other employment costs (benefits) must be included in the expenditures. Income from your personal savings, or investors does not count.

Without a crystal ball, it's impossible to determine exactly when you'll have positive cash flow, enough patients or clients to keep your business afloat, and whether you'll be able to purchase that yacht you have your eye on...

However... all else being equal, advocacy businesses starting up at this time in history are at a huge advantage. Between the numbers of advancing-aged baby boomers, the trend toward larger families (three children seems to be the new two!), and the confusion of healthcare reform, there can be no better time for such a business to develop.

11   http://bit.ly/finstmts

But the second reason you built those time frames was to give you intervals in which to measure your progress.

Here's an example: Suppose you determined in your first six months you would define your branding, print your business cards and a new brochure and launch your new website, plus begin gathering email addresses to send a monthly newsletter to. Further, you will have accumulated at least 50 of those email addresses and will have sent out your first newsletter, which will have resulted in at least one inquiry phone call for your services.

At six months, you'll want to go back to your plan to be sure you've accomplished all that. You'll want to see whether you are ahead or behind what you had planned. If you are ahead – bravo! If you are behind – then step it up!

Regardless of where you are, you'll need to make adjustments to your plan – again – in time frames. However, now your NEW six months will be one year from the start of your plan, your NEW one year will be 18 months after you started – but you'll be tracking and learning and adjusting.

Remember – your plan is a roadmap. If you somehow veer off your path, no matter what direction, you need to get yourself back on the right road. That's true with your marketing, too.

How Will I Know My Marketing Is Working?

There are actually a couple of indicators that your marketing is working – or not.

If your bank account is overflowing and you've got more business than you can handle – well that's one indicator that you're doing quite well.

However, it's possible your marketing is working, but it's not necessarily driving sales. In Chapter One, we looked at the difference between marketing and sales – short review: marketing is support to make sales happen.

Throughout this book, in particular the descriptions of tactics, we've talked about the many ways to track your marketing. As a reminder: by measuring the number of website hits just after you've run a newspaper ad, or asking people to ask for "Extension 5" or being interviewed by your local TV news crew after you did a PR push to encourage them to contact you as an expert.

If you continue to track those successes, and failures, too, you'll know which parts of your marketing are working. You'll even have an idea of what parts need to be adjusted.

If you don't get the results you want, then you'll know your marketing needs adjustment. You'll want to reread the sections of this book that apply. And don't forget, if your strategies aren't right to begin with, then your tactics won't work well anyway.

When Your Marketing Doesn't Increase Sales

Sometimes, despite your best efforts, your business won't grow enough. If you don't make that assessment early, then you may not recover enough to keep your business viable.

When you realize business isn't growing steadily, you'll need to assess what the reasons can be.   Understanding the underlying problem will help you right your course, as long as you do that early enough in the process—another reason to be reviewing and refining constantly.

Here are some of the reasons your business may not grow:

- **Your health advocate business may be too narrow.** An example would be an advocate who offers too few services, or the wrong services to the wrong group. We looked at marketing research in Chapter Thirteen. If you know there are enough people in your area who could possibly need your services, then it's possible they are finding some other alternative to get those needs met. For example, if your service is the ability to research diagnoses on the Internet, and you know that 10,000 people in your area are getting diagnosed with cancer each year, then you know those people are getting their information from someone else. If you are an exercise coach who works exclusively with pregnant women, then you may want to broaden your services to include post-partum exercising as well.

  Those alternatives are your competition and you need to understand your competition's USP in order to know how to get beyond it. Re-analyze your competitors and see if there is some way you can persuade them to be coopetition instead.

- **You may not have the background that people believe you need to do the work you are doing.** This has less to do with your business and more to do with you – but it may be possible to fix it by refining your business model.

For example, if you offer the ability to translate a doctor's appointment into words your patient can understand, and your potential clients perceive that you need a medical degree to do that well, then they may not want to hire you, believing you are not skilled enough to handle the work. (Remember - there's a difference between the reality of whether you can do that work, and the perception by your audiences about whether you can.) In a case like this, you might want to invite a doctor or nurse to be a partner in your business, then promote that – meaning – your target audiences' esteem of your company's abilities may rise.

- **There may not be enough of your target audience that understands what you do and how it can help them.** In this case, you'll need to put the education portion of your marketing work into high gear. Begin setting up speaking programs, plus other tasks we've discussed in earlier chapters.

- **You may be charging too much, or not enough, or your fee structure may not be well understood**. This is something you'll need to work out by educated guessing to begin with, and refinement over time. Learn more about figuring out what to charge in Chapter Fifteen.

- **You may not have given yourself enough time.** As business owners, we want to hang out a shingle, and have our calendars crowded within a day or two. It doesn't happen that way! You may need to develop some patience while your business grows.

Here are some of the marketing reasons your business may not grow:

- **Your strategy may not be well-constructed**. Go back to Chapters Two through Four and review how to build your strategy. If you feel as if you did a good job, then ask an outsider to review it for you – like the business development advisors mentioned earlier in this chapter.

- **You may have been too conservative in your marketing.** Too conservative may mean you have spent too little time on marketing tasks, or you haven't been willing to spend enough money on tactics you need outside help for. You'll want to increase your marketing efforts.

- **Your timing may be off.** Be sure you time your marketing pushes to fit the interests of your target audiences. For example, if you specialize in hospital bedside advocacy, you can do a nice PR push in June by focusing on the dangers of July hospitalizations. Doing that same push in May or August just won't work.

There are many more reasons a business struggles or fails. If none of these seem to fit, you can read more about those the SBA has cited as reasons businesses don't do well.[12] Asking a small business advisor to review your marketing plan with you is a great approach to identifying them.

. . . . .

One more important aspect of your marketing plan is yet to be tackled – the cost.

---

12   http://bit.ly/businessfailure

Chapter Fifteen
Time, Cost and Other Considerations for Your Marketing and Plan

We're almost there – a total marketing plan.

But one major consideration hasn't yet been made; that is, the cost in both time and money for executing your plan.

Budgeting for your overall business is a task you complete while developing your business plan. But marketing is – or at least should be – one of your major considerations in the development of your overall budget. So let's review some points that can help you determine how much money and effort you'll want to put into your marketing to be sure it's as successful as you want it to be.

How Much Business Do You Want to Attract?

If you responded, "All I can get!" then you may want to think again. Suppose your phone began ringing off the hook with new potential clients. Could you handle more than one or two new clients at a time? Would you want to turn anyone away? Probably not.

So a better answer to that question is, "Enough to fill my available time!"

Most health-focused advocacy work, at least those aspects that involve care (as opposed to insurance or billing) don't have the luxury of time. Unlike, say, a hairdresser who can tell you she's sorry, but she can't fit you in until a week from Thursday, most advocates find their services are needed immediately because a new diagnosis has just been declared, and treatment decisions need to be made, or because an older person needs assistance transferring to a new living arrangement – whatever it might be.

It becomes a challenge, then, to balance your marketing so that you acquire new clients in their optimum time frames. You want to be just busy enough – not too busy, and not under-scheduled either.

So how do we figure out what that will take?

Time is Money

Many new advocates come from the world of working for the government or a non-profit organization. Often that non-profit environment doesn't put the same premium on time as a for-profit business does. If that's true for you, then being in business for yourself is going to be a huge wake-up call, where you will need to learn to be efficient and effective at the same time, spending as little time as possible on non-moneymaking tasks in order to free yourself up for those billable hours.

If most of your experience has been in an environment where you worked for a salary that was not tied to the amount of work you complete in a given period of time, then it may take a while until you totally understand that time truly does equal money:

- *The more hours you work directly for your patients, the more money you will make.*

- *The less time you work directly for your patients, the less money you will make.*

- *If you don't work efficiently, it will require more time to do everything that needs to get done.*

- *Too much time spent working on non-income producing tasks means too little time to spend on the work that will produce an income.*

While all this may seem logical, it's a good reminder to everyone, even those who understand the time = money paradigm in business.

So we need to look at the cost of marketing in both those terms – money and time, too.

One approach is to **optimize your number of billable hours** – that is – the hours you spend working with patients that you will actually be paid for. Please note, that is not the same as the hours you spend working with patients. You may end up spending more hours than you anticipated on any given project, hours that you can't get paid for. In fact, in most service businesses, the number of real, billable hours is usually a fraction of the number of hours actually worked.

Some of that discrepancy can be controlled. For example, the way you actually price your work can affect your billable hours (project pricing vs hourly pricing, for example.) Also, as a general rule, the fewer actual clients you work with, the fewer non-billable hours you may work, too. For example, you won't spend as many hours doing administrative tasks like billing, or driving from location to location, if you work with three clients as you will if you work for five.

That said – don't limit your number of clients to too few either. Putting all your advocacy business eggs into only one or two patient baskets could be catastrophic to your business. You could lose all – or half- of your business the moment you lose a patient, no matter how you lose that patient.

There is no perfect formula, but you can approach the right answer by asking yourself a series of questions:

- How many hours per week or month do I want to be doing advocacy work (as opposed to administrative, running-your-business work)?

- How many clients do I need to provide that many hours of work?

- How many clients do I already have and how much time do they require from me?

- What amount of my current work will need to be replaced soon? (Do I see an end to the work I have with my current clients that will need to be replaced in the next 3 to 6 months? You may solve their problems, they may be cured, they may die or even move away.)

And then...

- What do I need to invest in marketing to make that happen?

Here's an example of how this line of questioning can help you. Say you have already been doing some advocacy work, but now you are formalizing a business and need some planning for this new business. Here's how you might answer those questions:

Work hours per week desired:	*35 billable hours (don't forget, some of your time each week will need to be devoted to the administrative business and marketing tasks that need to be done, too.)*
To fill 40 hours:	*3 full time clients @ 8 to 10 hours each* *2 part time clients @ 3-5 hours each*
Already have:	*Mrs. Smith = 10-12 hours* *Mr. Jones = 8-10 hours*
Will need replacing:	*Mr. Jones – 2-3 more months*
Need to market:	*Current needs: 20 hours/week*
	Future needs: 10 additional hours/week
Which equals:	*3 full time patients (or part time to make up the gap)*

Obviously, this questionnaire will change every time you gain or lose a client. But at least it gives you something to aim for.

So what force of marketing will it take to garner three new full time patients or however many patients will make up 30 hours-worth per week? And how much of your time will it take to rustle them up?

This is the point where you'll want to review your marketing plan to figure out which part of your arsenal you want to deploy. If you have been working with your marketing plan already, and have some of your tracking done, then you'll also have a good idea of which parts of your plan will be most efficient for rustling up those new clients or patients.

If you are just starting out with your plan, then you'll want to begin implementing the steps you think can bring you the most accurate return, the return that will fill your available space.

How Much Money Will It Cost to Keep Current Clients and Gain New Clients?

Different types of businesses attempt to suggest different percentages of a budget for marketing. A cable TV company might use 25% of its overall budget for marketing purposes. On the other hand, a lawyer might devote only 5% of her budget to marketing. Those numbers have been arrived at over many years, and using input from many similar businesses.

For health advocacy businesses, that approach can be problematic because most are so new, so we don't have a lot of track records to analyze. Further, it seems that advocacy businesses are either very small (one or two advocates), or they are larger corporations that hope to target big businesses to hire them to advocate for their employees. We have no rules of thumb.

If someone backed me into a corner and told me I couldn't be let out until I threw out some dollar amounts, then I might take a wild, but educated guess at those costs...

Here is where I would begin:

- Start Up Marketing Costs: $5000.

- Ongoing Marketing Costs in Year 1: $1000 per advocate working for the enterprise

- Ongoing Marketing Costs after Year 1: $1000 per advocate working for the enterprise

What will that money buy you? In the first year, it will buy you some time with a marketing consultant who can help you build your plan. It will also buy you a rudimentary website and some other tactics you may want to pay for – those #1s in Chapter Six, the ones you've built into your marketing plan.

In subsequent years, it will help you reassess what's working, and will add additional tactics to help you grow your business.

How Much Time Will It Cost to Keep Current Clients and Gain New Clients?

When you first begin your business, or during the planning stages, you may feel as if you have all the time in the world to devote to marketing. But as business picks up, and you find yourself with more and more billable hours, then you'll realize that your time spent with marketing needs the double E's just like everything else: effectiveness and efficiency.

And yes, time equals money.

How much time you spend on executing your marketing tactics will be a function of the time you need to fill with billable hours, too. If your client roster is full, you'll still want to do some marketing, but you won't need to spend nearly the amount of time as you will if your week has some hours to fill with billable work.

A simple answer to the "how much time" question is this: If you aren't staying busy with billable hours, then you aren't doing enough.

Here's another rule of thumb:

Early in the building of your business, try to spend 10 to 12 hours a week on your marketing. This will include networking, branding and plan assessment (all discussed in earlier chapters.) This will help you establish your business's reputation and will help you bring in new clients, too.

Once you have a full client roster, you'll still want to spend 3 to 5 hours per week on marketing tasks. This work will be mostly marketing maintenance work, and will be based on your review of what you've been doing to that point, and the tracking of successes and failures.

How Will You Know What to Charge for Your Services?

While the "what should I charge" question is not really a marketing question, it has a definite place in this conversation. However, the question of what to charge is impossible to provide a blanket answer for because each health advocate does different work, and resides in a different locale. However, I can give you some guidelines for honing in on your fee structure.

If you have competition (other exercise coaches or midwives in your area, for example) try to find out what they are charging. It doesn't hurt to call and ask. You can even ask a friend to call and ask.

Once you know what they are charging, you can look at what you want to charge in two ways. You can charge a bit less, hoping people will choose you based on price, and thinking they are getting a better deal. Or you can charge a little bit more, focusing on your USP (unique selling proposition which you developed in Chapter Three.) Remember the old maxim, "You get what you pay for." Often people will think you are worth more just because you, yourself, are valuing your services in a higher plane.

Here's a story that illustrates what I'm talking about:

Many years ago, my neighbors' schnauzer, Lucy, got loose one afternoon. While on the lam, Lucy and Zeke (my family's cocker spaniel) rendezvoused.... About two months later, Lucy gave birth to a half-dozen "schnockers" – as cute as they could be.

But the neighbor didn't want to raise six schnockers, so she ran an ad in the newspaper: "Free to a good home." The phone never rang.

After giving it some thought, the neighbor realized that if the puppies were free, then people might think there was something wrong with them. She was putting a value of nothing on them, when, in fact, they were really quite adorable.

So she ran a second ad, and this time put a price tag of $50 on them. Her phone rang off the hook. She could have sold dozens of schnockers!

And so it is with your services. Don't undervalue them. If you do decide to charge more than your competitors, just be sure your first several clients feel like your extra touch was worth the extra expense, and garner testimonials from them to prove it.

If you don't have competition (maybe no one else in your area is offering the same services you'll offer) than it will be tougher to determine what you should charge, but it can still be done.

First, ask some people you trust what they would be willing to pay for your services. Give them a few scenarios that fit the work you do, and the circumstances your potential clients will be in. (Such as, "You have a heart attack, and your son can't get here from out of town for three days – what would you pay to have someone sit by your bedside to keep you safe while you are in the hospital?" Or "You have three different specialists you see on a regular basis, and they all keep prescribing drugs for you, but your primary won't take the time to review your drugs. What would you pay someone to do that review for you?")

Provide as many scenarios as you can (as they are patient enough to help you with!). And ask as many people as possible the same questions.

At the same time, contact other advocates who do similar work to your list of services that aren't competitors, usually because they are located in other cities or states. They may be willing to share their pricing with you because you aren't competitors.

Now take into consideration what your trusted friends have suggested, average them out with what your non-competing but similar advocates have told you – and start your pricing from there.

As long as you don't publish your prices anywhere, then you can even let them fluctuate from client to client while you assess your comfort level in what you are charging.

When I started my marketing company back in 2001, I was offering some web services unlike the way anyone had offered them before. What I've just described is exactly how I started. Further, I used different pricing structures with different people, based on how much I thought they would be willing to pay for my services. I found myself raising my prices on a regular basis until I was charging more than I ever thought I could!

A wise business advisor once told me that you'll know you are pricing yourself successfully when you are charging more than you ever thought you could, but you still have as much business as you can possibly handle. I got there. You will, too.

(You can find far more pricing information, including how to do the math to figure out what to charge, in *The Health Advocate's Start and Grow Your Own Practice Handbook*. See the Resources in the back of this book.)

Don't Ever Stop Marketing

And so we've covered the basics of marketing for health advocates. From strategies to tactics to tools. From budgeting time, cost and pricing. Soup to nuts.

No doubt, over the years as your business grows, you'll develop some great strategies and tactics not mentioned here. If you're willing to share them, I'd love to hear about them!

You'll also find that some go by the wayside, perhaps not working well for you, or over time, for anyone. Just a few years ago I would have suggested you send lots of postal mail postcards to potential clients. But today, for most health advocates, that makes no sense.

I would wish you luck, but I don't really believe much in luck. Seneca, a philosopher from the 1st Century AD, is credited with saying "Luck is the point at which preparation meets opportunity."

Your opportunity for succeeding as a health advocate starts today. And in building your marketing plan, you'll be well prepared. That's all the luck you will need.

Sure! Go ahead!
This is a blank page, and it's
your book, so make some notes...

Chapter Sixteen
Resources

Find additional resources by chapters here.

If you prefer to link to any online resources directly (rather than inputting this text), you can find them hotlinked from the book's website: HealthAdvocateResources.com/HABMH

Chapter One:

Small Business Administration | www.sba.gov

The Alliance of Professional Health Advocates | Dozens of tips and other support for members of this organization: www.APHAdvocates.org

Chapter Three:

To be notified of credentialing programs for patient advocates: | Sign up for updates—see the form on the right at: www.AdvocateCredential.org

General marketing advice: | http://marketing.about.com/ About.com

http://www.entrepreneur.com/marketing/index.html Entrepreneur Magazine

Business.gov US government

For members: www.APHAdvocates.org

Coming mid-2014: | The Health Advocate's Advanced Marketing Handbook

Sign up to be notified of publication: www.HealthAdvocateResources.com

Chapter Four—Branding

Branding basics   http://marketing.about.com/od/brandstrategy/u/
                               brandbasics.htm

Psychology of colors   http://www.color-wheel-pro.com/color-meaning.html

Type / fonts   http://en.wikipedia.org/wiki/Serif

Chapter Eight—Public Relations

Press release format   http://HealthAdvocateResources.com/HAMBH

HARO—Help a Reporter Out   http://helpareporter.com
Pitch Rate   http://pitchrate.com

PR Web   http://PRweb.com
PR Newswire   http://PRNewswire.com
PR Free   http://PRFree.com (most services are not free)
Free Press Release   http://Free-press-release.com

Setting up News Alerts in   http://bit.ly/newsalertsetup
Google or Yahoo

Online newsletters—email   http://iContact.com
address management
                               http://ConstantContact.com

                               http://MadMimi.com (this is the service used by APHA)

Chapter Nine—Advertising

Pay Per Click—Using Adwords   http://www.google.com/adwords/
on Google

Magnetic Car Signs   http://www.buildasign.com/MagneticSigns
                               http://www.wholesalemagneticsigns.com/
                               http://www.bestgraphicsimage.com/

Chapter Ten—On the Web

AdvoConnection and the Alliance of Professional Health Advocates

For Advocates	http://APHAdvocates.org
For Patients	http://ww.AdvoConnection.com

Register your URL	http://GoDaddy.com
	http://Register.com
	http://NetworkSolutions.com

Applications for building websites include:	InDesign (Adobe)
	Dreamweaver (Corel)

Online applications for building websites	Homestead: http://www.homestead.com/welcome/
	Moonfruit: http://www.moonfruit.com/
	Weebly: http://www.weebly.com/
	Wix: http://www.wix.com/
	Yola: https://www.yola.com/

Submit your website to search engines	Google: http://www.google.com/addurl/?continue=/addurl
	Yahoo: http://search.yahoo.com/info/submit.html
	Bing: http://www.bing.com/webmaster/submitsitepage.aspx

Google Analytics	http://www.google.com/analytics/ (you will need a Google account)

Starting a blog— instructions	http://patients.about.com/od/socialnetworking/ss/How-To-Start-A-Health-Or-Medical-Blog.htm

Online Support Groups	http://www.dmoz.org/Health/Support_Groups/

Chapter Twelve—Miscellaneous Tactics

Gift idea: You Bet Your Life! The 10 Mistakes Every Patient Makes
                              (How to Fix Them to Get the Health Care You Deserve)

                              http://YouBetYourLifeBooks.com
                              Bulk pricing is available.

Surveys   www.surveymonkey.com

                              www.polldaddy.com

Chapter Thirteen—Building Your Marketing Plan

Demographics for research   http://quickfacts.census.gov/qfd/index.html

Marketing Plan Template   Can be found in the linked resources at:
                              www.healthadvocateresources.com/HABMH

Chapter Fourteen—Reviewing and Refining Your Plan

Small Business Administration   http://www.SBA.gov

SCORE—Service Corps of   http://www.score.org/index.html
Retired Executives

SBDCs—Small Business   Do a search engine search using SBDC and your state
Development Centers

Financial Statements   http://www.entrepreneur.com/article/159786

Reasons for business failures   http://bit.ly/businessfailure

General Information

Much more information about the business of advocacy and marketing for advocates can be found in these resources:

www.HealthAdvocateResources.com

Organization:
The Alliance of Professional Health Advocates for currently working advocates and those who wish to explore career possibilities.

These workshops are held throughout the year in cities across the US

Subscribe to let potential clients know of your ethical business practices.

The APHA Blog showcases current thinking, business tips, useful resources and more.

Patients and caregivers find advocates to help them in the AdvoConnection Directory

About.com

Find dozens of articles about patient empowerment and patient advocacy at About.com Patient Empowerment

The Health Advocate's Marketing Handbook makes marketing your advocacy services far easier than you might think.

The Health Advocate's Start and Grow Your Own Practice Handbook is a step-by-step guide to geting you started in your own private advocacy practice.

These special reports are available only for short periods of time.

Currently:

Your Annual Health Advocacy Practice Checklist 2014

Coming Soon!

The Health Advocate's Advanced Marketing Handbook

From advocacy degees and certificates, to a calendar with current learning events, you can find opportunities for courses and training here.

Patients and caregivers can ask questions. Advocates suggest solutions.

You Bet Your Life! can teach you about the way the healthcare system works, and how to work around the problems to get what you - or your clients - need.

About the Author

When Trisha Torrey was diagnosed with a rare, aggressive lymphoma in 2004, she was a marketing consultant who knew almost nothing about healthcare. She was also naïve to the dysfunction of the American healthcare system that was tasked with treating her.

But she got smart, fast. She learned that the possibility of excellent care was too easily and frequently eclipsed by miscommunication and mistakes. She also learned that if she didn't stick up for herself, and insist on the help she needed, she would not get it. The more empowered she became, the more she realized there was a possibility she had no lymphoma. Eventually she proved she was right; she had no cancer.

Once Trisha put that "no cancer" odyssey behind her, she decided it was up to her to apply her skills to teaching others how to navigate the dangerous landscape of American healthcare. She sold her marketing company in 2006 to devote herself full time to the cause.

Today Trisha calls herself "Every Patient's Advocate." She is the founder of AdvoConnection.com and the Alliance of Professional Health Advocates which support the business aspects of a health advocate's work. In addition, she About.com's expert in patient empowerment and advocacy, speaks to groups of patients and professionals, and teaches workshops. She is the author of four books: *You Bet Your Life! The 10 Mistakes Every Patient Makes (How to Fix Them to Get the Health Care You Deserve), The Health Advocate's Start and Grow Your Own Practice Handbook,* this book, and *The Health Advocate's Advanced Marketing Handbook* (coming in 2014.)

Trisha has been quoted by CNN, the Wall Street Journal, O Magazine, U.S. News and World Report, NPR, Scientific American, Angie's List Magazine, Bottom Line Publications, and others.

She lives in Central New York State with her husband, Butch, and her mini-mutt, Crosby. When she's not doing her patient advocacy thing, she enjoys playing golf, travel, gardening, and working in stained glass.

Twitter:	@TrishaTorrey
LinkedIn:	www.LinkedIn.com/TrishaTorrey
Google+:	http://gplus.to/trishatorrey
About.com:	http://patients.about.com

DiagKNOWsis Media

www.DiagKNOWsis.com

DiagKNOWsis Media is the umbrella formation for all patient and advocate activities developed by Trisha Torrey since 2004. It includes:

The Alliance of Professional Health Advocates
http://APHAdvocates.org
And blog located at: www.APHAblog.com
This is a membership site for health advocates which provides business support, including marketing support.

AdvoConnection for Patients
www.AdvoConnection.com
A website that helps patients and caregivers search for a professional advocate. Those advocates listed are members of the Alliance of Professional Health Advocates.

The Health Advocate's Start and Grow Your Own Practice Handbook
www.HealthAdvocateResources.com/SGOP

Just as it is named, this book is written specifically for those who wish to start their own private, independent advocacy practice, and grow it once it's off the ground.

Purchase of this book also includes a one month free trial membership in the Alliance of Professional Health Advocates.

Health Advocate Resources
www.HealthAdvocateResources.com

Find more than one dozen resources to help you become recognized as an independent advocate—books, websites, educational programs, code of standards and more.

You Bet Your Life!
The 10 Mistakes Every Patient Makes (How to Fix Them to Get the Health Care You Deserve)
www.YouBetYourLifeBooks.com
Trisha's first book helps patients, caregivers and advocates better understand the healthcare system and point of view, then uses that understanding to provide tools and tactics to help them improve their medical system outcomes. Available from the books' website, or through online retailers (Amazon, BN, Borders). Bulk pricing is available.

Every Patient's Advocate
www.EveryPatientsAdvocate.com

And blog, located at: www.TrishaTorrey.com

DiagKNOWsis Media
www.diagKNOWsis.com
This is the main website for DiagKNOWsis media and provides a listing of all DiagKNOWsis activities.

Index

Personal Case Examples of being ocp pt adv

Eric - asthma/pneum

CM Examples

Elevator - I own Hag HC founded in 2014. We provide consulting services to payors+ provider groups, ~~hospitals~~ comm. agencies who are seeking ~~an independent, corper~~ external expert advice regarding medical management strategies to

Unlike the national big consulting firms like   , as an ~~independ~~ boutique consulting company, we can deliver more efficiently solutions at lower costs. Often. big firms hire indep. consultants

Made in the USA
San Bernardino, CA
15 August 2015